Water Moves the Color
Reflections on the *Dao De Jing*

Galen Pearl

Photos Lydia Pallas Loren, Galen Pearl, and Martha Spence

Also by Galen Pearl

*10 Steps to Finding Your Happy Place
(and Staying There)*

I Speak to All Just So

Your Breath is Your Guru

© 2024 Galen Pearl, Lydia Pallas Loren, and Martha Spence
ISBN 978-0-9858462-7-5

Preface

Having spent over half a century with the *Dao De Jing*, including over a decade with the original Chinese, I had resolved never to provide the world with yet another translation of this ancient wisdom teaching. My reasons were simple. I had discovered in the Chinese characters a mysterious and marvelous multiplicity of meanings that flowed beautifully like a mountain stream, ever changing, ever pure, ever beyond capture, much like Dao itself.

But then these two wonderful women approached me about making this book, wanting to match their evocative photos with the text. Immediately, my reluctance floated away like dandelion seeds on a puff of breeze, proving once again the impermanence of everything in the manifested universe.

So here is my humble offering. I claim no superiority in translation, nor any scholarly acuity in reflection. I have simply tried to convey something of what the *Dao De Jing* reveals to me in this moment, knowing that its vast wisdom is beyond any attempt to define or explain its elusive truth. I hope I have failed well.

This book is an invitation, welcoming you into contemplation of words and images to inspire your own discovery of the innate wisdom that dwells forever within your being. Enjoy.

Introduction

Although the origins of the *Dao De Jing* are lost in the mists of history, partial manuscripts date back to the 3rd century BCE. And although the author is named Lao Zi, that simply means "old master" and does not identify a specific individual. Scholars have debated origin and authorship for centuries, and while that inquiry is intriguing, it does not obscure the poetic beauty and profound wisdom held in roughly 5,000 Chinese characters, which have been organized into 81 chapters.

In translating the text, I have left a few words in Chinese because there just isn't a single word in English to convey the breadth and depth of meanings contained in certain characters and how they are used in this teaching. The variations in translating even the title of the *Dao De Jing* are evidence of this.

"Dao," often translated as way, can mean path, like a path you walk on or a path you take in life. It can mean the way things are or the way we do things. And it can mean the ineffable, mysterious way of the universe.

"De" is often translated as virtue, which can be misconstrued as a structured code of morality. It is also sometimes translated as power, but again this can be misconstrued as power over things or people. The virtue of De is the innate integrity within each of us that aligns us with the natural order of Dao in the universe. The power of De is likewise the inner power of Dao that moves through us and out into the world when we are in harmony with our true nature.

"Jing," by the way, simply means a classic or sacred text.

I have also refrained from translating "qi," which literally means vapor, steam, or breath, and is often translated as vital energy or life force.

It's no wonder that the *Dao De Jing* is one of the most translated texts in the world. The multiple and fluid meanings of the characters result in as many variations as there are people who undertake this predictably challenging yet surprisingly satisfying endeavor. In joining their ranks, I have used several manuscripts and classical Chinese resources to explore the characters and meanings that, to me, capture the rhythm, poetry, beauty, and wisdom of this mysterious message that speaks to us across the ages.

Chapter 1

The eternal Dao cannot be explained
The eternal Name cannot be spoken
The nameless is the origin of heaven and earth
The named is the mother of ten thousand things
Ever desireless one sees the essence
Ever desiring one sees the manifestation
These two are one yet perceived as different
Within this oneness is deep mystery
Deep and ever deeper
The door to all marvelous wonder

Chapter 1 Reflections

Ah, the beauty of this chapter brings me to tears. Each line is its own fertile ground for endless contemplation. Together, they hold all the wisdom in the entire text of the *Dao De Jing*. Beyond the limits of language and thought, the truth of this chapter shines radiantly and eternally.

So what can we do but pause in quiet awe of what is inexplicable and nameless, and then talk about it! As the author does for 80 more chapters and as writers have done over centuries in countless books.

The chapter starts off acknowledging the elusive nature of Dao, which confounds the rational mind that we in Western culture are so fond of. We like to analyze, label, and categorize, so that we can create a logical structure that we call reality. The idea that there is reality beyond what our minds can grasp does not sit well with some. And yet this chapter invites us to step into the ethereal dance between the origin of heaven and earth, and the mother of ten thousand things.

This is the interplay between undifferentiated essence and manifestation from that essence into form, both aspects of the creative energy of the universe. Empty of desire, our inner vision reveals the mystery. Desire turns our attention to the beauty of the sensory world. Some find an implied judgment, suggesting that being without desire is somehow better, but I don't think so. This chapter tells us that the essence and the manifestation are one. In oneness, how can there be judgment? That would be like saying that undifferentiated light is good, but light refracted into the colors of the rainbow is bad. It's all light.

That mountains of words have been written about this first chapter alone might imply that the chapter is inordinately complicated, when, at least to me, it is elegantly simple. But its simple beauty is accessible only when we reassure our nervous minds, busy trying to figure everything out, that all is well. It's okay not to have a name for everything. It's okay not to know, to sink ever deeper into the mystery until we enter the gateless gate of infinite expansion.

The Universe said, "Let me show your soul something beautiful."

~Aberjhani

Chapter 2

Under heaven all perceive beauty in relation to ugliness
All perceive goodness in relation to what is not good
Being and nonbeing give birth to each other
Difficult and easy complement each other
Long and short shape each other
High and low support each other
Sound and voice harmonize each other
Therefore the sage abides without interfering
Following the teaching beyond words
Allowing the ten thousand things to arise without judgment
Creating without possessing
Acting without expectation
Completing work without claiming credit
Without attachment nothing is lost

Chapter 2 Reflections

The Biblical creation story begins with the earth formless and empty, not barren but brimming with infinite and undifferentiated potential that manifested into forms as God called them forth. In this way, heaven was separated from the earth, the waters from the land, and the dark from the light. What was one became many, all distinct parts of the whole.

Likewise, we see in this chapter the manifestation of the ten thousand things from the formless and empty void of Dao. What we might perceive as opposites are in reality connected concepts, identifiable only in relation to each other. I demonstrated this once with three sticks of different lengths. Holding up two of them, I asked which stick was short. Then I took the short stick and held up one even shorter. The stick that was short just a moment before was now the long stick. What we think of as inherent qualities are often revealed to be dependent on relational context.

The illusion of opposites is even more apparent when we add judgment into the mix. I don't think it's a coincidence that the one tree in the Garden of Eden that was forbidden was the tree of knowledge of good and evil. Quite apart from any religious significance, one can see that a lot of suffering results from becoming attached to such distinctions.

No wonder, then, that the sage is aligned in harmony with the fluid movement of energy in the universe, recognizing the interrelatedness of everything, allowing all things to be as they are, without need for personal gain or acclaim. The character for sage 聖 shows an ear and a mouth on top with the earth underneath, suggesting that the sage listens and speaks grounded in, and supported by, the wisdom of the natural world.

Perhaps when we understand the illusion of opposites, there is no longer a need to judge things as good or bad, no need to force things to conform to our wishes. We can develop a sense of nonresistance, an ego-free attitude towards life, a respect for the natural harmony and wisdom of the universe and for our place in it.

As long as words are used to denote a truth, duality is inevitable; however, such duality is not the truth. All divisions are illusory.

~Yaga Vasistha

Chapter 3

Exalting some above others causes contention
Prizing rare or costly goods causes theft
Coveting what we desire causes disturbance
Thus the sage governs
By emptying the ego and filling the belly
By quieting the mind and strengthening the bones
Without cunning and craving
The wise refrain from interfering
Acting without attachment
All is in order

Chapter 3 Reflections

Bellies and bones! This chapter presents a very embodied image of nonattachment. The three opening examples highlight the relationship between perceiving disparity and the resulting discord. All three examples – exalting some above others, prizing rare or costly goods, and coveting what we don't have – illustrate placing value on something through our own judgment, a value that is not inherent in the thing itself. That value creates distinctions, leading to desire and attachment.

This doesn't mean that we no longer have wants or preferences. Even the Dalai Lama admits to a fondness for gadgets. He tells a story of seeing something shiny in a display window of an electronics store and wanting it, even though he didn't know what it was for. We like some things; we don't like other things. We might feel pleased to have something or disappointed not to have something else. The difficulty arises, however, when we hold our happiness and well-being hostage to things we've attached subjective value to.

The sage is one who recognizes this. The section describing how the sage "governs" is often interpreted as guidance for governing others. I prefer to view this passage in reference to how we govern ourselves.

I love the poetic imagery of filling the belly and strengthening the bones. Ego and attachment occur mostly in our thoughts, in our minds. Thus emptying the ego and filling the belly doesn't mean sitting down to a super-sized meal, but rather allowing our awareness to sink from up in our thoughts to down in our center. The Yellow Emperor called this "swallowing the breath of heaven." We can access this energy physically by breathing into our bellies, relaxing our abdomen and allowing it to expand naturally as we breathe. Figuratively, filling our bellies breaks the energy loose when it is stuck in thought loops in our minds and allows it to move freely and easily throughout our whole being.

Likewise, quieting the mind and strengthening the bones doesn't mean heading to the gym, but rather being so perfectly aligned in our literal and figurative structure that we move with little or no effort through our lives because we are in harmony with the universe.

With a "full belly and strong bones," we are well able to maintain our inner peace through alignment and nonattachment. In this way, all is in order and life unfolds naturally. Everything moves in harmony and we flow effortlessly along our way.

Practice experiencing everything in a state of non-expectancy and non-attachment. The beauty of living will suddenly become clear.

~Steve Leasock

Chapter 4

Dao's great emptiness pours forth an endless abundance
From its bottomless abyss emerge the ten thousand things
Its deep pool of tranquility is forever present
I know not from whence it comes
It existed before the gods

Chapter 4 Reflections

This short chapter, one of my favorites, and one of the most enigmatic, evokes the mysterious, profound nature of Dao by using three images. The Chinese characters for these images all contain a water component, even though their meanings are not specifically water related. It's like the characters themselves illustrate the fluid quality of Dao. Indeed, water is the element most closely associated with a description of Dao and is the most frequently used metaphor to convey the essential nature of this elusive concept.

冲 *Dao's great emptiness pours forth an endless abundance*

The first image is a character meaning emptiness, like a hollow bowl or an empty vessel. The emptiness of Dao is not barren but is dynamic with infinite potential. The character also has a connotation of welling up, like an inexhaustible spring bubbling up from the ground. The three little lines on the left side represent water. The right side means center or middle. How intriguing to contemplate the "center of water" in connection with the image of an empty cornucopia of abundance.

渊 *From its bottomless abyss emerge the ten thousand things*

The second image is a character meaning bottomless depth, like an abyss. Again we see the water component on the left side, while on the right side the three vertical lines mean river, with rice in the center, emphasizing the fertility as well as the fluidity of Dao. The "ten thousand things" is a phrase used in the *Dao De Jing* to represent the manifested universe, the world of countless forms. Dao is often described as the origin of creation and the source to which all things return in an endless cycle of formlessness emerging as form and returning to formlessness.

湛 *Its deep pool of tranquility is forever present*

The third image is a character meaning profound tranquility, not in a stagnant way, but in the sense of a deep, still pool holding infinite energy in its mysterious darkness. Beside the water component on the left, there is a component on the right meaning extremely or to the greatest extent, emphasizing the vast mystery of Dao.

I love this chapter because the water metaphor is hidden in the characters, hidden and yet right there in plain view, like Dao itself. Think for a moment about water's qualities. It doesn't struggle. It flows around obstacles. It can't be grasped. It yields to force (think of your hand pushing through water), yet nothing is stronger (think of the Grand Canyon). It follows the laws of gravity, not exerting energy, but simply flowing downhill unconcerned about its route or its destination. It changes appearance—liquid, solid, vapor — yet never loses its true nature. How can I be guided by water's wisdom in my own life?

Be water, my friend.
~Bruce Lee

Chapter 5

Heaven and earth are impartial
Viewing the ten thousand things as straw dogs
The sage is impartial
Viewing all people as straw dogs
The space between heaven and earth
Breathes like a bellows
Empty yet not lacking
Producing without end
Words have their limits
Better to abide in the center

Chapter 5 Reflections

The opening of this chapter is one of the most misunderstood passages in the *Dao De Jing*. To some it seems harsh, but deeper reflection reveals the beauty hidden within.

The characters used here for impartiality are sometimes translated as ruthless, heartless, or without kindness. Such cruelty or moral judgment is not aligned with the text as a whole, so it's hard to reconcile such interpretations with the overall themes of harmony and fluid effortlessness in the *Dao De Jing*. Instead, I understand this concept of impartiality as the same lack of favoritism reflected in other wisdom teachings.

For example, the Bible says: *He makes his sun rise on evil and good, and sends rain on the just and unjust.* And Buddhist teacher Thich Nhat Hanh likewise speaks of the generosity of a flower that shares its fragrance and beauty with all passersby without judgment or preference.

Even in martial arts, the concept of "having no preference" is key to being fully present and able to respond appropriately to whatever is happening in the moment. This is just as true in our everyday lives. This is not an impartiality of cold, uncaring detachment, but rather the impartiality of an engaged open heart, welcoming all without distinction or reservation.

The other term often misconstrued in this opening passage is straw dogs. Straw dogs were objects used in sacred rituals, and afterwards discarded. Some view this reference as suggesting that the ten thousand things, including people, are not important. However, the value of straw dogs was not in their form, which was recognized as impermanent, but in their function, which was holy. All things living on this earth will die, and their forms will disappear, but their impermanence does not render them meaningless. The cycle of living and dying, like the cycle of breathing, is the ongoing energy of all creation. So while a particular form comes into being for a time and then returns to the source, the cycle of life itself continues unchanged in the eternal expression of creation.

The sense I get from this chapter is of equanimity, remaining balanced in the center of life's vicissitudes, showing kindness and compassion to all, recognizing the sacredness of everything.

Nothing here below is profane for those who know how to see. On the contrary, everything is sacred.

~Pierre Teilhard de Chardin

Chapter 6

The valley spirit never dies
Known as the dark mare
Whose womb is the root of heaven and earth
Forever and ever birthing all of existence
Effortlessly creating worlds without end

Chapter 6 Reflections

If Chapter 4 is one of the most enigmatic and Chapter 5 is one of the most misunderstood, then Chapter 6 is one of the most poetically beautiful. And one of the shortest. Just 26 characters, it has spawned pages upon pages of commentary. Like the blind men and the elephant, everyone sees different facets of meaning. When we can release the need to have a single "right" meaning, when we can let the meanings swirl in fluid undulations, then we enter the true meaning beyond words, the mystery beyond understanding. And it is sublime.

The valley spirit is an image often associated with Dao. The valley is open, receptive, fertile, representing the feminine energy of yin. Like the image in Chapter 4 of the empty vessel that is never exhausted but always dynamic with potential, the valley sustains and nurtures with unending abundance, vibrating in symphonic harmony with the ten thousand things.

I love the imagery of the dark mare. The character for dark can also mean mysterious, unknown, profound, and carries a sense of translucence, allowing light to pass through without revealing form. The character for mare can mean female and also womb. Metaphorically, these characters carry forward the concept of the fertile valley in the first line, a place of gestation, the mysterious source of life. This is not life in the abstract, but life of the earth, the dark, rich soil in which seeds split and germinate and reach toward the light as their roots burrow deep.

"Forever and ever" is represented by the character 绵 used twice for emphasis, doubling the eternal aspect of creative movement. The root or radical of this character is on the left side and means silk or silk thread. In taiji and qigong, we are taught to move energy as though reeling a silk thread. Silk thread is delicate yet strong, but if you jerk or force it, the thread will break. The movement of creation, like reeling silk, is fluid, spiraling, cycling, and powerful.

The poetic imagery of this chapter invites us into the mystery of life, the vibration of creation, the amazing miracle of it all.

There are only two ways to live your life. One is as though nothing is a miracle. The other is as though everything is a miracle.

~Albert Einstein

Chapter 7

Heaven is eternal and earth long lasting
This is so because they are unborn
Thus they exist forever
Therefore the sage stays behind yet is ahead
Is unattached to self yet ever present
Ever without self-concern
The sage is self-fulfilled

Chapter 7 Reflections

This short chapter uses some reference to "self" seven times, inviting us to consider our concepts about ourselves: who we are, what we are, and how we relate to the rest of creation. How is our concept of "self" different from the eternal aspect of heaven and earth? How is being "unborn" relevant to existing forever?

We typically think of ourselves in terms of our bodies, our personalities, our identities. We have a history, a narrative of our lives and a list of attributes that we identify with. These are all unique qualities that come into existence as we are born and grow, and are extinguished at death. Without denying that, is it possible that we are also something more, something that is beyond our individual birth and death?

The largest living organism on the planet is a mushroom fungus that spreads over several square miles in eastern Oregon. When I first learned this, I pictured an enormous mushroom towering over forests and valleys like something out of a science fiction movie. The mushroom fungus is actually an underground network of fibers connected over an area as a single organism. What we normally think of as a mushroom is in fact the fruit of the mushroom fungus. Individual fruits pop up here and there and they seem to be separate, but they are all connected to each other through this underground network. We don't see the true mushroom; we see only the fruits.

Is it possible that we, like that single mushroom organism, exist as part of an infinite network of being? Our individual egos are born and die, like the mushroom fruits, but the essence of who we are is vast, eternal, and singular. Thus, as the chapter teaches, those who understand this have no need to promote themselves or be concerned with individual achievement. Because of this, they live in harmony, content, fulfilled.

This is not a teaching of self-sacrifice and denial as much as it is a teaching of liberation and transcendence. Of awakening. Of coming home. The price of the ticket, from the ego's perspective, is everything, which is what makes it seem so scary. But when we awaken, we realize that what we thought was everything was nothing at all. The ticket is free because all we give up is the illusion that we are limited by our temporary manifestation as an individual fruit of infinite and eternal creation.

What the caterpillar calls the end of the world, the master calls a butterfly.
~Richard Bach

Chapter 8

The highest good is like water
Water's goodness benefits the ten thousand things without striving
It flows to the low places shunned by people
And thus remains close to Dao
A good home is in harmony with the earth
A good heart is deep beyond measure
Good relationships are nurtured by kindness
Good words are sincere
Good leadership is just
Good work is skilled
Good action is well-timed
Just as water does not strive
And is therefore without error

Chapter 8 Reflections

Water is the most common metaphor for Dao in the *Dao De Jing*. Chapter 4 used several characters to describe Dao that had water radicals or roots. Here the chapter begins by explicitly comparing Dao to water. But just as significant in this chapter is the character for good or goodness 善. Used nine times, it invites us to explore the relationship between the image of water and the concept of goodness.

We often think of goodness as something we do, something we aspire to, even something to be. We want to be a good person and do good things. We internalize a standard of goodness, sometimes adopted from some external source, against which we measure ourselves, often judging ourselves for falling short. So we try harder.

This chapter, however, paints a very different picture of goodness. Here we see goodness as the natural expression of Dao. It flows effortlessly like water, nourishing all creation without striving. It yields to gravity, flowing into the low places that people may avoid, yet this is where it meets the highest good of Dao. This reminds me of Jesus, who sat not at the high table with powerful rulers, but at the low table with common people.

When we are aligned with Dao, goodness naturally manifests in all aspects of our lives. We live in harmony with the earth. Our hearts are open to give and receive an inexhaustible abundance of love. Our thoughts, words, and actions are all expressions of goodness, not because we are striving to be good, but because we are allowing the inherent goodness of our true nature to flow unimpeded.

When we remain close to Dao, we can trust that we will be carried on the current of creation's natural perfection, without harm or mistake.

Trust in the Lord with all your heart, and do not lean on your own understanding. In all your ways remember him, and he will make straight your paths.

~Proverbs 3:5-6

Chapter 9

Better to stop pouring before the cup overflows
Better to stop sharpening before the edge is too thin
A hall piled with treasure cannot be protected
Self-importance and pride are the path to misfortune
Work is accomplished, the self does not matter
This is the Dao of heaven

Chapter 9 Reflections

I think of this chapter as the "sweet spot" chapter. Or in a more light-hearted vein, the Goldilocks chapter, since it emphasizes not going to excess beyond that "just right" balance. I also appreciate the humanness of this chapter. I suspect that there is something in here that each of us can relate to.

The first line reminds me of the professor who went to visit a Zen master. The professor, who considered himself an expert on Zen, pontificated while the master quietly poured tea in the professor's cup. When the cup was full, the master kept pouring until the tea spilled over onto the table and then to the floor. The professor finally interrupted his lecture to exclaim, "Stop! The cup is full. No more will go in." The master replied, "You are like this cup. You must empty yourself before you can learn."

When we fill our minds with opinions and judgments, especially high opinions of ourselves and judgments of others, there is no room for genuine connection or dialogue.

Many of us can identify with the caution against oversharpening a blade. We occasionally catch ourselves overthinking a decision or a problem until our head hurts and a solution seems even further away. But when we stop and set it aside, an answer comes directly into our awareness.

But my favorite might be the caution against hoarding treasures. I don't have a lot of gold and jade, but I do love books. How many more do I need? Maybe just one more….

The warning against self-importance and pride echoes the Bible's observation that pride goes before destruction and a haughty spirit before a fall. Why is pride so bad and self-esteem so good? Pride separates us from others. It isolates us by placing us, in our own minds, above others. It closes our hearts and spirits to the wisdom of the universe that is equally available to all. Self-esteem, on the other hand, allows our true nature to manifest. Because we are neither puffed up nor insecure, we are liberated to be our authentic selves, naturally connecting to others in the vast tapestry of life.

When we heed the advice in this chapter, we do not force or grasp. We simply do what needs to be done and release our attachment to the outcome. We are aligned and in harmony with the Dao of heaven, perfectly balanced in the "sweet spot."

In the beginner's mind are many possibilities,
but in the expert's mind are few.

~Shunryu Suzuki

Chapter 10

Embracing the oneness of universal spirit and individual soul
    We can be without separation
Focusing the breath gently
    We can be like a newborn babe
Purifying deep insight
    We can see without obstruction
Caring for people or governing a country
    We can act without interfering
Engaging with the vicissitudes of life
    We can remain open and receptive
Attaining enlightenment
    We can understand without knowing
Create and nurture without possessing
Act without taking credit
Lead without dominating
This is profound De

Chapter 10 Reflections

What a perfect chapter for uncertain times, a guide for living perfectly in an imperfect world. Here we are introduced to the concept of De, sometimes translated as virtue, not in the moralistic sense, but more in the sense of a natural integrity which manifests organically in alignment with Dao. I think of it like fruits of the spirit described in the Bible, such as love, joy, peace, kindness. Fruits of the spirit are not some externally imposed requirements of morality. They are "fruits," growing effortlessly in the fertile ground of surrender to the Holy Spirit.

Likewise, De is not separate from Dao, but rather is the natural expression or revelation of Dao in the world. De can take many forms, just like life manifests as the ten thousand things, everything appearing different yet sharing the universal energy that breathes life into all things. In the same way, all forms of De make visible an inner power and harmony that radiate from Dao like the rays of the sun.

We can further understand De by contemplating the Chinese character.

德

The top right component 直 (with the vertical rectangle turned horizontally to fit in the character) means straight or upright in the sense of upstanding. It is in turn made up of ten 十 eyes 目, suggesting an all-seeing vision. Underneath that is the component meaning heart, suggesting clear vision centered in the heart. The left side of the character 彳 means stepping forward. When we put this all together, we have an image of De as going forward in our lives guided by the inner vision or wisdom of the heart.

And what would that look like? This chapter describes the "fruits" of De that arise naturally when we are aligned with Dao, arising as effortlessly as an apple grows on an apple tree. Trusting and following the inner guidance of the heart's wisdom, we live in harmony, acceptance, connectedness, integrity, and compassion.

But the fruit of the Spirit is love, joy, peace, forbearance, kindness, goodness, faithfulness, gentleness and self-control.

~Galatians 5:22-23

Chapter 11

Thirty spokes meet at the hub
Yet the hole in the center makes the wheel useful
Clay is molded to form a vessel
Yet the emptiness within makes the vessel useful
Doors and windows are cut to build a house
Yet the space within makes the house useful
We value what is there
But we use what is not there

Chapter 11 Reflections

This chapter highlights the often overlooked essential quality of emptiness. We tend to focus on the form around the emptiness rather than on the emptiness itself. In my home, for example, I have a lot of original tilework around the doors and windows in the kitchen and bathroom. It's beautiful, and people often comment on it. But the doors and windows are meaningless without the open space outlined by the tiles. I've read that in parts of ancient China, homes were sometimes carved out of cliffsides. So rather than creating a home by enclosing space, like we usually do, they created homes by emptying out space. In other words, they didn't create the form; they created the emptiness.

Emptiness plays a big role in martial arts. A teacher once told me to go into the empty space around my partner rather than to try to force him out of the space he occupied. He pointed to my partner's arm. "He is already here. Don't go there. Go where he isn't. Grow into that empty space like a tree." By moving effortlessly into the empty space, I left my partner nowhere to go. Also, by creating a sense of empty space within myself, my partner had no place to attack.

This chapter invites us to consider the usefulness of space, both external space around us, and internal space in our hearts and minds. When we contemplate space, we might become aware of our urge to fill it up! What is that about? Is there some hidden judgment about space as useless instead of useful? How many of us feel uneasy, for example, when we have empty space in our busy day? Is it ever useful to just do nothing?

If we observe our relationship to space, we might discover that space is not only useful but essential. When my mind is too full of thoughts and information, there is no space for clarity and wisdom. If I am talking too much, I can't have a conversation with someone because there is no space to listen. If my heart is full of judgment, there is no space for love. If my spirit is too full of beliefs, there is no space for faith or trust. If I am too attached to my narratives of life or my identity, there is no space for my life to unfold naturally. One of the spaces we most like to fill up is silence, but we need the space of silence to hear the song of the universe within us.

Maybe we can go on our own version of an astronaut's space walk. We might spend a little time exploring space in our lives, looking past the form to the usefulness of both external and internal emptiness.

The moment you are not, enlightenment is. With emptiness, the matter is settled.

~Osho

Chapter 12

The five colors blind the eye
The five tones deafen the ear
The five flavors dull the taste
Galloping on the hunt inflames the heart
Chasing rare goods hinders wise action
Therefore the sage is guided from the center in the belly
And not by transient distractions of the eye
Attachment is thus easily avoided

Chapter 12 Reflections

One might read this chapter as condemning enjoyment of sensory pleasure in life. As I write this, I'm looking out the window at a rainbow array of spring flowers. I'm listening to birdsong carried on breezy rays of warm sunshine wafting through the open door behind me. I readily admit to enjoying these pleasant sensations. Is that wrong? I don't think so. In fact, sensory surveys and sensory integration are used in various therapeutic contexts with great benefit. So what is the message here?

Perhaps we are being cautioned not against appreciating beauty in this amazing life, but against getting so distracted by superficial cravings that we are unable to hear our inner guidance and align ourselves with it. Buddhism teaches us that attachment, not enjoyment, is the cause of suffering in this world. Attachment, like craving, takes place in the mind. We place value on something, we want it, we set out to get it. If we fail to get it, we are unhappy. If we do get it, we might be happy for a time, but then we are afraid to lose it and find our happiness slipping away.

All the while, as we are galloping off to chase imagined treasures, we are missing the experience of what is actually happening in the present moment. In that sense, our eyes are blind, our ears are deaf, and our taste is dulled. When, on the other hand, we are fully present with our whole attention on what is, everything is revealed to us in truth. Grounded and centered within, we are not buffeted or hooked by the mind's "shiny object" distractions of judging, craving, rejecting, or spinning out narratives. We are free to enjoy all of life's delights without agenda or attachment.

I'm reminded of lyrics from two songs which, to me, represent the message of this chapter:

> *Oh Lord, won't you buy me a Mercedes Benz?*
> *My friends all drive Porsches, I must make amends*
> *Worked hard all my lifetime, no help from my friends*
> *So, oh, Lord, won't you buy me a Mercedes Benz?*
>
> ~Bob Neuwirth and Michael McClure

All that I am
All that I see
All that I've been and all that I'll ever be
Is a blessing
It's so amazing
And I'm grateful for it all, for it all

~Nimo Patel and Daniel Nahmod

Chapter 13

Honor and disgrace relate to fear
Fortune and calamity relate to self
How do honor and disgrace relate to fear
Honor brings one down
Having it makes one fearful
Losing it makes one fearful
Thus honor and disgrace relate to fear
How do fortune and calamity relate to self
Both arise from attachment to self
Without attachment to self
Fortune and calamity are without meaning
When self-interest extends to all creation
All creation is cared for as the self
When self-love extends to all creation
All creation is embraced as the self

Chapter 13 Reflections

Unlike many chapters that use only a few characters to generate lots of meanings, this chapter uses a lot of repeated characters to convey a very simple message about equanimity. Equanimity requires a certain degree of detachment. This doesn't mean not engaging with life. It doesn't mean not caring about anything. It means not getting hooked by the stories others tell about us or the stories we tell ourselves about our circumstances. It means not struggling against the natural flow of impermanence that is reflected in the human condition.

What we detach from can be external or internal. Honor and disgrace originate externally from what others think of us. Both can cause us to be fearful because they depend on what we can't control. When we give others power over our well-being, we can never be at peace.

Fortune and calamity originate internally from our own judgment about our circumstances. The story is told of a poor old farmer who had a son and a horse. When the horse ran away one day, a neighbor exclaimed over the farmer's misfortune since without his horse he could not farm his land. The farmer calmly replied, "Who knows if it's good or bad?"

The next day the horse returned leading twenty wild horses. The neighbor congratulated him on his new wealth. The farmer shrugged with the same reply. The next day the son broke his leg trying to tame one of the wild horses. The neighbor bemoaned his ill luck. You know what the farmer said. The next day the army swept through the village, taking all the young men away to fight...except the son with the broken leg.

You get the idea. When we are able to detach from our own judgments, as well as from what others think, we reach a state of unshakable equanimity and remain at peace as we navigate the currents of our lives. Equanimity does not remove us from the experience of life. On the contrary, our engagement with life is expanded and deepened as we experience our natural connection with all creation, caring for it all, loving it all, grateful for it all.

There is a huge amount of freedom that comes to you when you take nothing personally.

~Don Miguel Ruiz

Chapter 14

You can look but you will not see it
Its name is mystery
You can listen but you will not hear it
Its name is silence
You can grasp but you will not catch it
Its name is emptiness
These three elude investigation
They are woven into oneness
From above it is not bright
From below it is not dark
From in front there is no beginning
From behind there is no end
It expands infinitely beyond description
All things return to its embrace
Within its formlessness is all form
Its vastness defies imagination
Align with timeless Dao
To empower present existence
From the beginning to this moment
Dao's thread connects all creation

Chapter 14 Reflections

If you can understand it, it's not God.

~St. Augustine

This quotation, to me, best represents the analysis-defying beauty of this chapter. The Sanskrit expression "neti, neti," meaning "not this, not this," says even more simply that ultimate truth can't be organized, labeled, or described. Indeed, the Chinese character 不, meaning no or not, appears nine times in this chapter.

The unfathomable mystery of Dao is revealed in this chapter not only by the language used, but also by the fluid lack of structure. There is no separation of distinct thoughts. Lines of characters can be grouped in different combinations to give different meanings, as evidenced by the wide range of translations. It is, as one commentator noted, the language of the mystics. Despite eluding understanding, or rather because of it, we are invited by the rhythm and swirling symmetry of the Chinese poetry to let go of solid ground and enter the mists of the infinite.

The language is beautiful. But what does this mean to us in our daily lives? In one sense, it means nothing. The nature of mystery is that it doesn't enter our rational minds in some concrete, practical way. Instead, it calls us to transcend the mundane to enter, as a 14th century monk named it, the cloud of unknowing. From there, our lives become less about in-*form*-ation, and more about in-*spir(it)*-ation. When we are attuned to that inspiration, it breathes into and permeates our daily lives. And in that sense, it means everything.

For the things that are seen are transient, but the things that are unseen are eternal.

~2 Corinthians 4:18

Chapter 15

Ancient masters of Dao were
Subtle, mysterious, profound, penetrating
Like deep water they were unknowable
Recognized only by their demeanor
Careful, as crossing a winter stream
Alert, as aware of surroundings
Courteous, as a guest
Yielding, as melting ice
Simple, as uncarved wood
Empty, as a valley
Opaque, as murky water
Murky water through stillness becomes clear
Stillness through movement becomes life
Those aligned with Dao stay in balance
They seek nothing for themselves
And thus move through life fulfilled

Chapter 15 Reflections

Followers of Dao are as elusive and mysterious as Dao itself – mystics, living in the liminal space between being and nonbeing, movement and stillness, yin and yang, manifesting and returning. We are told that they cannot be known or understood, yet the author gives us a description of their demeanor – careful, alert, courteous, yielding, simple, empty, opaque. These qualities are not cultivated independently, but rather are the natural expression of alignment with Dao. And alignment can be cultivated.

The chapter gives us a helpful image in cultivating alignment, that of an uncarved piece of wood 朴. The image of uncarved wood is used to convey not only simplicity but also unlimited potential. Before it is carved, a block of wood can become many things. It represents the beginner's mind of Zen.

How can we live with beginner's mind? As we mature, we make choices that set us on certain paths at the exclusion of others. As we age, we realize that some choices are no longer open to us. What does it mean to have beginner's mind amid life's commitments and limitations?

To me, the focus of beginner's mind is internal rather than external. After all, the term is beginner's "mind," not beginner's "life." No matter our circumstances, we can engage with life with a mind that is open, curious, eager, courageous, connected, willing. Perhaps this is what Jesus meant when he said that we must become like children to enter the kingdom of heaven, not childish but childlike, greeting every day afresh with wonder.

Beginner's mind aligns us with Dao in a natural, fluid relationship. When we are aligned, we live in harmony with this rhythm, our individual identity begins to soften, and we become one with the dance of all creation. In nature, there is no separation. Nothing exists in isolation. Everything belongs in the interconnected web of existence.

When we live in alignment with Dao, we, like the ancient masters, are fully aware as we engage with each precious, present moment. Our daily lives are not escaped but transformed, and we find ourselves living with the unlimited potential and promise of that uncarved wood.

For today, newly bright.
~title of painting by Cecilia Lin

Chapter 16

Empty yourself of your self
Abide in perfect tranquility
As you watch the ten thousand things take form
And return to formlessness
Returning brings serenity
Serenity restores our destiny
Our destiny remains constant
Knowing this is enlightenment
Not knowing this brings suffering
Knowing this leads to open mindedness
Which leads to generosity of spirit
In alignment with eternal Dao
Although the impermanent self fades away
The eternal Self remains unharmed

Chapter 16 Reflections

What begins in time ends in time. Everything that manifests into form will return to formlessness. Every aspect of the created universe will arise into being and return to nonbeing, including us, or at least the temporal aspect of us. We are born into form and our form will return to "the dust of the earth."

Buddhism teaches that everything is impermanent. Everything that lives will die. But life itself does not die. My body will age and die. The ego that I think of as myself will cease to be. But the spark of life within me is eternal. From this perspective, we can abide in perfect tranquility as we watch the ten thousand things emerge into form and return to formlessness, as unerringly as salmon return from the sea to the waters in which they were spawned.

It sounds so serene, but life on the ground doesn't always feel so tranquil. Kids are misbehaving, the power goes out on a cold day, we're stuck in traffic, our dog is sick, we're angry about something. Tranquility is hard to find in difficult circumstances, especially if we are judging ourselves for not being tranquil!

The Chinese character 静 used for tranquility and serenity in this chapter gives us some guidance about how to abide in tranquility in circumstances that might not be serene. The left side of the character is a component that means a blue green color, with a calm, soothing, quiet connotation. The right side of the character, however, means strife or conflict, not something you would expect in a character meaning tranquility. To me, this suggests that tranquility is not the absence of strife but has more to do with our attitude towards the inevitable challenges of life. We can't always change what is happening in our lives, but we can change our relationship to what is happening.

When things are feeling chaotic or overwhelming at home, my friend and her partner look at each other and say, "Living in the eye, baby!" We find tranquility not by escaping from challenges, or denying them, or judging them, but by going right into the center of them, being fully present without struggling, at peace in the eye of the storm.

When I look within and see that I am nothing, that is wisdom. When I look without and see that I am everything, that is love. Between these two, my life turns.

~Nisargadatta Maharaj

Chapter 17

The highest ruler is barely known
Next is one loved and honored
Next is one respected yet feared
Next is one defied and scorned
Who lacks sufficient trust is not trusted
The highest ruler chooses words carefully
Work is completed and tasks carried out
The people together say
It happened naturally

Chapter 17 Reflections

Enlightened leadership is a theme throughout the *Dao De Jing*. Often, as in this chapter, the characters used to denote leadership could refer to a ruler, a government, or an individual's self-management. In any context, however, the hierarchy is clear, moving from what is barely known to what is honored, then feared, then scorned.

When distilled to this essence, the levels below the highest all involve some kind of judgment. Honor, fear, and scorn are all based on an evaluation of something as good or bad. But the top level of being barely known is neutral. When leadership operates in harmony with Dao, it leads without forcing or imposing its power on others. The best teacher, for example, is one who empowers and inspires students to take responsibility for their learning rather than dominating them and keeping them dependent. The teacher leads by remaining in the background.

Likewise, if referring to how we "govern" ourselves as individuals, we might recognize these qualities of natural self-confidence at one end of the spectrum and brutal self-condemnation at the other.

Trust is central to this chapter, literally in the middle line of the chapter, and figuratively as the quality that enables the harmonious dynamic between the leader and the led, whether referring to governments or ourselves. Fear and force arise in the absence of trust, foreclosing the possibility of a healthy, productive relationship.

This chapter invites us to explore our own style of leadership. Do we lead with a light touch or with a heavy hand? What part does trust play in how we lead ourselves and others?

Enlightened leadership fosters a sense of community and interrelatedness. Life unfolds organically, naturally, harmoniously. What needs to happen, happens. We need not make ourselves the center of the narrative. Just for fun, I tried to recount my day without using a first-person reference. I found this very challenging! My tendency to make myself the subject of my life reveals to me those places where I try to direct or control. But when I am able to get myself out of the story, I can begin to see the natural rhythm of my life, and of life in general. My account went something like this:

*Laundry is done. Grandson helps fold towels. There is teaching and playing.
Laughter fills the room. Towels are put away.
Hearts are full of love.*

Chapter 18

When great Dao is forgotten
 Kindness and morality arise
When intellect and knowledge emerge
 Nature gives way to great artifice
Loss of family harmony
 Leads to filial piety and parental commitment
When the nation is unsettled
 Loyal ministers appear

Chapter 18 Reflections

This modest little chapter does nothing less than represent the entire debate between Confucianism and Daoism, two major philosophical traditions arising at approximately the same time in ancient China. With apologies to scholars and philosophers for my oversimplification, Confucius taught that conscious cultivation of identified virtues leads to personal, social, and governmental harmony. The *Dao De Jing*, in contrast, teaches that when we live in harmony with Dao, these virtues naturally manifest without deliberate effort.

In simplest terms, it's a question of direction. Confucianism starts from an external moral structure that through internal conforming leads to an ordered society. It's characterized by obedience to fixed rules of social norms. Daoism starts from internal alignment with Dao that organically manifests in external harmony. It is intuitive rather than rule-based, fluid rather than fixed, and emphasizes alignment over obedience.

One might ask if it makes a difference since either way, you end up with positive qualities for individuals and communities. But while kindness, morality, filial piety, and loyal ministers are good things, they are, in the absence of internal alignment with Dao, imposed rather than natural, and thus reflect "great artifice" rather than "great Dao." Artifice has a negative connotation, but the character 偽 breaks down into the left part meaning person and the right part meaning action, and can simply mean man-made. Man-made has a more neutral feeling, something that originates from the self or ego. That doesn't make it bad, but it can lead to separation from the intrinsic order and harmony of the universe.

I'm reminded of the Bible story of the tower of Babel. Briefly, a bunch of people got together and decided to build a tower high enough to reach heaven. They failed, showing that union with God (the universe, whatever name you want to use) is not reached through artificial means. In the present day, I wonder about the development of "artificial" intelligence and "virtual" reality. Again, this doesn't mean they're bad. They are like the artificial light we turn on when the sun goes down. It is man-made and useful when we have lost the natural light, but maintaining the artificial light requires a great deal of effort and expense, with far reaching consequences. Despite its essential role in modern life, it cannot duplicate or replace the sun, which shines effortlessly and for free on all the earth.

My soul can find no staircase to Heaven unless it be through Earth's loveliness.

~Michelangelo

Chapter 19

Abandon saintliness discard wisdom
People will benefit a hundredfold
Abandon benevolence discard morality
People will return to harmonious relations
Abandon shrewdness discard profit
Thieves and bandits will disappear
Therefore follow these teachings
Understand simplicity embrace purity
Reduce self-interest temper desire
Abandon learning be at peace

Chapter 19 Reflections

Abandoning saintliness and wisdom reminds me of a Zen center I visited years ago. The monk who led this group seemed to make a point of being "unsaintly." He would walk around in his black robes with a cigarette in one hand and a glass of wine in the other, but I never saw him actually smoke or drink. I wondered if he did this to discourage his followers from idealizing him as some kind of holy guru. Irreverent and funny, he was unfailingly kind and generous, with a twinkle in his eye and a deep love of everything. His followers, on the other hand, floated around with beatific smiles while appearing, at least to me, to try to outdo each other in enlightened behavior. We are so human, aren't we?

If we abandon benevolence and morality, which many consider to be the bedrock of civilized society, what's to keep us from devolving into chaos and violence? On the other hand, how well has adherence to a moral code of justice worked for humanity so far? The *Dao De Jing* teaches that when there is internal resonance with the natural order of creation, there is a spontaneous manifestation of beneficial qualities as the reflection of the basic goodness of the universe without need for an enforced code of behavior.

And what would happen to our capitalist economy if we renounced shrewdness and profit? I'll leave that to others to sort out. But in its simplest form, I think the principle here is not to take advantage of others, and not to grasp greedily for things that we crave more than we care about the things that really matter, which, perhaps not surprisingly, are things that cannot be grasped, greedily or otherwise.

The teachings in the last three lines could be read individually, as six separate encouragements. Alternatively, they could be read as linked concepts, which is my preferred interpretation. In this view, understanding simplicity naturally sheds the unnecessary, which allows pure perception to emerge. As we see things more clearly, we are less concerned with self-interest and our desires are less compelling. And as our cravings are quieted, we are not so driven to know all the answers, and our anxiety dissipates into peace.

Beware lest you lose the substance by grasping at the shadow.

~Aesop

Chapter 20

Abandon learning be at peace
Yes and no
Good and evil
Are they really different
Fear generates more fear
A wilderness without end
People are all excited
As if celebrating spring festival
I alone appear quiet as an unborn child
Empty, belonging nowhere
People all have plenty
I alone appear left out
People all have purpose
I alone differ from others
Rolling like an ocean wave
Gentle as an endless breeze
Content to be nourished by the Great Mother

Chapter 20 Reflections

This chapter begins with a line that ended up being a joke on me!

Abandon learning be at peace

There is much scholarly debate about the placement of this line. Some place it here at the beginning of this chapter. Others place it at the end of the last chapter. There are good arguments on both sides. After spending a lot of time studying expert commentary and doing my own analysis of alternative placements, I felt flummoxed and frustrated by the lack of a definitive answer. Then I sat back and laughed. Oh right, abandon learning and be at peace.

I quit worrying. The wisdom of the line was clearly and effectively demonstrated through my own futile attempts to determine its correct placement. The line, like Dao itself, can float where it will. With that in mind, I let it float in both places, at the end of the last chapter and at the beginning of this one. I am at peace. How perfect that the line that stumped me regarding its placement was teaching me through direct experience the truth of its words.

Through several examples, the rest of the chapter contrasts the follower of Dao, that is, one who embraces the wisdom of the opening line, with people in general. By comparison with folks who are going about their busy lives pursuing intellectual knowledge, acquiring possessions, devoting themselves to an established role in society, the follower of Dao appears isolated, simple, without ambition or direction.

This description might sound negative, but taken in context, it represents with undifferentiated formlessness of origin, or, as named by an anonymous Christian mystic, the cloud of unknowing. When we enter this cloud, we leave rational thought behind. We abandon learning, and there, in that cloud of mystery, is where we meet God. Or, as the last line of the chapter says, we are nourished by the Great Mother.

When we remember this, as the first line promises, we have no anxiety. We live in trust. Like the lilies of the field and the birds in the sky, we are created and sustained by an energy we call by many names but is beyond names and understanding. It is not ours to know, but to have faith. And when we can allow that flower of faith to bloom, we rest peacefully in the perfection of being.

When we trust the universe, we open ourselves up to the infinite possibilities that life has to offer, and we invite in the magic and mystery of the unknown.

~Bernadette Logue

Chapter 21

The vast presence of De in the world
Exists entirely as an expression of Dao
Dao is elusive, murky, mysterious
Yet within its elusiveness is substance
Within its murkiness is form
Within its deep mystery is life's essence
Within life's essence is perfect truth
From the beginning until now
The eternal name has remained unchanged
Thus we experience Dao in all of creation
How do I know
By this

Chapter 21 Reflections

This chapter describes the connection between Dao and De. As noted before, De can be loosely translated as virtue, not in the moralistic sense, but more in the sense of inner harmony or integrity. It's what Dao "looks like" in the manifested universe. It *is* Dao *as* the manifested universe.

Chapter 1 told us that "the nameless is the origin of heaven and earth; the named is the mother of ten thousand things." There is creative power in naming something. In the Biblical creation story, God brought forth form out of formlessness by naming. When he said, "Let there be light," there was light.

Here we see De as the named aspect of Dao, which is beyond names. De emerges from Dao as the ten thousand things, the entirety of the manifested universe. I think of it like twinkling stars being birthed from a star nursery. The murky, undefined cosmic cloud is brimming with primordial, undifferentiated star "stuff," out of which appear countless sparks of light, individual stars. To me, this is a most magnificent and magical image of form arising from formlessness, the vast presence of De emerging from the cosmic cloud of Dao.

We can't see the wind, but we know it by its effects – by the feel of it on our skin, by seeing it push the clouds, by hearing it sing through the treetops. Likewise, we can't know unlimited Dao with our limited minds, but we can recognize the manifestation of Dao through the natural order and powerful beauty of creation. We know Dao by knowing ourselves, for we are an integral part of that creation.

As the Bible says, we are fearfully and wonderfully made. We often forget that we are magnificent, not because of individual qualities or achievements, but because we exist, each of us as a unique part of an integrated whole, inextricably woven into the fabric of everything that is now, ever was, and ever will be.

Dancers come and go in the twinkling of an eye, but the dance lives on.

~Michael Jackson

Chapter 22

Surrender becomes perfection
Crooked becomes straight
Empty becomes full
Worn out becomes renewed
Lack becomes gain
More becomes misleading
Therefore the sage embraces one
And becomes the model under heaven
Not self-absorbed thus enlightened
Not self-asserting thus illustrious
Not self-boasting thus accomplished
Not self-arrogant thus respected
Because the sage does not contend
There is nothing for others to contend against
Thus it is said surrender becomes perfection
Restoring all to wholeness

Chapter 22 Reflections

Surrender becomes perfection

If the first line of this chapter is the only one you read, it is enough. Three words...so simple. But within them is the path to awakening, the key to liberation, the secret of the vast power of the universe that manifests through all of us when we release resistance. As Adyashanti says, "Surrender is the name of the spiritual game."

We sometimes think of surrender as humiliating defeat. In the spiritual context, however, it means to cease struggling against reality, a battle no one will ever win. Furthermore, unlike defeat in war which can lead to oppression, surrendering the futile struggle against reality opens us up to liberation and the cessation of suffering. Yes, reality is sometimes painful, but our wanting things to be other than they are only increases suffering by keeping us unbalanced and out of harmony. Our resistance will not stop creation's endless cycle of becoming.

Surrender does not mean being a doormat or not responding to our world with courage and integrity. On the contrary, surrender is the ultimate courageous practice, and will leave us stronger and better able to engage appropriately with whatever arises in our lives. This is reflected in the passage about the sage who is not self-absorbed and thus manifests the qualities of an enlightened being. These are not qualities of weakness and defeat; they are qualities of triumph and power, not our personal power, but the infinite power of the sacred universe.

Because the sage does not struggle or contend, no one can effectively use force in return. This reminds me of a scene in the movie *Redbelt* in which a new martial arts student expresses anxiety about being injured. The teacher stands directly in front of her and asks, "If I'm standing here and you are standing there, can I hurt you?" "Yes!" she replies, to which the teacher calmly responds, "Then don't be there."

This good advice is represented in the character 争 meaning to contend or struggle. It looks top heavy, matching the rising energy of distress. And it stands on a single, unstable point, suggesting that struggle pulls us off balance. In contrast, the character for wholeness or perfection 全 suggests energy moving downward to rest on a firm base connecting heaven and earth in balanced harmony. From this stable position of balanced harmony, we enter the current of life's natural unfolding and we are at peace.

Grant me the serenity to accept the things I cannot change, the courage to change the things I can, and the wisdom to know the difference.
~Reinhold Neibuhr

Chapter 23

Speaking little is natural
Fierce winds do not last the morning
Torrential rains do not last the day
If heaven and earth cannot sustain such energy
Then how much less can we
Thus followers of Dao become one with Dao
Followers of De become one with De
Followers of loss become one with loss
Those joined with Dao are welcomed by Dao
Those joined with De are welcomed by De
Those joined with loss are welcomed by loss

Chapter 23 Reflections

Nature seeks balance and harmonious resonance. There is a natural rhythm of manifesting and returning throughout all creation. Everything has an intrinsic vibration that resonates in harmony with everything else. This is represented by the characters 自然 in the first line. The literal meaning is something like "self so," and refers to the spontaneous unfolding or flowing energy of nature in its totality and in all its unique aspects.

Heaven and earth cannot sustain indefinitely the intensity of stormy weather. Calm will be restored. Likewise, sustaining an effort to impose our will on other people or circumstances depletes our energy. Sometimes I am overly fond of words, especially my words. Like the fierce winds referenced in the chapter, my penchant for talking too much exhausts not only myself, but also my overtaxed audience. Just ask my kids. I should have the first line of this chapter taped to my mirror.

The natural inclination of heaven and earth towards balance and harmony is reflected in the passage about the paths we follow. Our own vibration seeks to harmonize with a corresponding vibration in the universe, and vice versa. Thus, when we follow Dao, we are one with the infinite potential of the formless, pregnant void before it births the ten thousand things of the manifested universe. When we follow De, we are in harmony with the natural flow of energy in the world. We embrace rather than fear the fluid perfection of impermanence.

Even when we follow the path of loss, forgetting our true nature, trapped in ego, the path of loss harmonizes with our choice, and we become identified with the illusion of a separate self. There is no judgment here, or punishment. There is simply vibrational resonance. Our ego consciousness keeps us in a state of forgetfulness until we wake up and remember who we are.

This chapter calls our attention to the natural harmony of the universe and reminds us that we have the power to choose our path through life.

The goal of life is to make your heartbeat match the beat of the universe, to match your nature with nature.

~Joseph Campbell

Chapter 24

One who stands on tiptoe is not steady
One who straddles cannot move forward
The self-absorbed are not enlightened
The self-righteous are not illustrious
The self-praising are not accomplished
The self-important are not enduring
One who follows Dao
Sees these as excessive and extraneous
All beings avoid them
Therefore those aligned with Dao move on

Chapter 24 Reflections

The wisdom of the first two lines describing physical positions is demonstrated in martial arts practice. If my energy is not grounded or centered, I become unbalanced and I'm easily uprooted. Moreover, if my energy is divided equally in both feet like a straddle stance, it is difficult to move fluidly.

As in martial arts, so in life. Fear, anxiety, anger, any emotion that makes us feel churned "up" will cause our energy to rise. Breathing becomes rapid and shallow in our upper chest instead of slow and deep in our belly. We feel emotionally off balance and unsteady.

The second line about straddling reminds me of how we sometimes feel when we're stuck trying to make a decision. We often go back and forth in our thoughts, weighing pros and cons, or perhaps we seek advice from various sources. Lacking clarity, we imagine possible scenarios, hoping one will start flashing in neon "right choice"! All the while, with all the mental noise, we cannot pause to listen for and hear the quiet, assured voice of our inner wisdom.

Both of these emotional positions, on tiptoes when we are churned up or straddling when we are hurrying to make a decision, mostly involve our thinking ego minds, isolating us in our mental gyrations, concerned for our self-interest in one way or another.

The middle passage exploring self-concerns mirrors a similar passage in Chapter 22, suggesting that this is an important lesson worth repeating, and emphasizing that alignment with Dao allows us to move through our lives fluidly and effectively. We are not confused because we trust that our way will become clear. We do not force and therefore have no conflict. We have no fear and therefore act appropriately and with confidence. We are unconcerned with credit or blame and therefore are unburdened. Our hearts are rooted in Dao and therefore our spirits are free to soar.

I never saw a discontented tree. They grip the ground as though they liked it, and though fast rooted they travel about as far as we do.

~John Muir

Chapter 25

Something mysterious, unformed, yet whole
Existing before the beginning of heaven and earth
Tranquil, unimaginably vast
Solitary, unchanging
Ever manifesting yet never depleted
The mother of all under heaven
Knowing not its name
I call it Dao
Or simply call it great
Its greatness expands throughout creation
And from infinity returns to the source
Permeating heaven, earth, and humanity with perfection
All realms of creation reflect its greatness
Humanity follows the earth
Earth follows heaven
Heaven follows Dao
Dao follows its intrinsic nature

Chapter 25 Reflections

The opening passage describes so beautifully the indescribable, unknowable nature of Dao. It reminds me of Genesis 1:2 – Now the earth was formless and empty, darkness was over the surface of the deep, and the Spirit of God was hovering over the waters. Throughout the *Dao De Jing*, the image of water gives us a sense of the nature and power of Dao. Dark, mysterious, fluid, feminine, Dao is the formless origin of all creation, the life-giving energy of manifesting into form, and the cycle of returning to the source.

It is unchanging in its limitless potential, yet the life that emerges from it and returns to it is ever moving, ever changing, ever impermanent. We see this cycle of manifestation and return reflected in everything around us – birth and death, the seasons, day and night. The most immediate and personal example is our breath, cycling through inhalation and exhalation, receiving breath by breath the life energy of creation, and then releasing it to receive again. Science tells us that the universe is expanding. I wonder if at some point it will cycle back and return, like a single breath of creation spanning eons.

My favorite character in this chapter 寥 means vast, empty, formless, beyond limits, silent. The top part of the character means roof; the lower part means the sound of wind, or soar. The lower part can itself be divided into two parts meaning feathers and long hair. The sound of wind reminds me again of the breath, and perhaps echoes the Hebrew name of God, YHWH, which I'm told cannot be pronounced and sounds like breathing, connecting us to the sacred with every breath. How magnificent.

The upper part meaning roof provides a sense of shelter, safety, protection, reminding me of the psalmist's promise that "He will cover you with his feathers. Under his wings you will find refuge." As our spirits soar with limitless freedom, we are ever held in the vast embrace of infinite love.

Breathing in, I smile. Breathing out, I release.
Breathing in, I dwell in the present moment.
Breathing out, I feel it is a wonderful moment.

~Thich Nhat Hanh

Chapter 26

Heavy is the root of light
Stillness masters restless movement
Thus the sage can travel all his days
Never straying from his true self
Even facing glorious sights
He soars above as a swallow flying free
What benefit to rule ten thousand chariots
If the self is not aligned with all under heaven
Then lightness loses its root
And restlessness roams ungoverned

Chapter 26 Reflections

Heavy is the root of light
Stillness masters restless movement

This opening couplet captures the essence of this chapter and reflects a life principle shared by martial arts and many wisdom teachings. Here, heaviness and stillness are not the opposites of, or balanced by, lightness and movement. On the contrary, they are the foundation on which lightness and movement rest. When we allow our energy to sink in stillness, our energy moves fluidly and freely.

One of my favorite examples of this principle comes from Greek mythology. Anteaus was the son of Mother Earth. As a warrior he was undefeated. His secret was the strength that he got from his mother. As long as he was in contact with the earth, no harm could come to him. In certain martial arts, we learn to root our energy in our feet in a way that maintains our balance and structural integrity. Thus grounded, we find an inner stillness from which movement manifests naturally, and we are not easily overcome by someone else's efforts. Indeed, taiji is sometimes described as "stillness within movement, movement within stillness."

This applies just as effectively in our daily lives. We often feel buffeted and sometimes overwhelmed by the chaos of life. We try to impose control through effort, thinking that our peace will come from managing our circumstances, instead of seeking first our inner stillness. With inner balance and harmony established, our way forward is clear and we move forward undisturbed and undistracted by whatever is going on around us.

This is demonstrated so perfectly by the character for stillness or tranquility 静. The character is made up of two components, 青 on the left meaning a soothing, blue green color, and 争 on the right meaning conflict or striving. You can see that the conflict component stands unsteadily on a single point, but it is balanced and supported by the component on the left. This suggests that tranquility is not dependent on our external circumstances, which are sometimes challenging, but rather on the calming influence of our internal stillness.

Next time you sense a "disturbance in the force," (thank you *Star Wars*), allow your breath to sink into your belly. Feel your feet on the earth and imagine roots drawing energy into your body. Like Anteaus, we are nourished and protected by our connection to our origin, to the life-giving energy of creation, to the sacred wisdom and power of the universe.

Serenity is not freedom from the storm, but peace amid the storm.
~S. A. Jefferson-Wright

Chapter 27

Good walking leaves no trace
Good words do no harm
Good analysis relies not on divination
A good closure needs no locks
A good bond needs no rope
Thus the sage quietly helps all people
Without judging anyone
And artfully releases attachment to all things
Without rejecting anything
This is called cloaking oneself in enlightenment
Thus the skilled teach the unskilled
And the unskilled are valued by the skilled
Without esteem for the teacher
And love for the student
Great wisdom is lost
This is called marvelous essence

Chapter 27 Reflections

The character 善 appears in this chapter eleven times, providing the central theme in this passage. It can be translated as good or skilled, and here describes actions in accordance with inner guidance or moral alignment. It means something closer to harmonious and integrated rather than goodness opposed to bad or wrong.

The first line reminds me of the '70s TV show *Kung Fu*. In the opening sequence, the young Shaolin novice trains for years to walk across delicate rice paper without tearing it. Because of the connotation of skill in the repeated use of 善, some people think that the focus is on ability attained through diligent practice. Indeed, the Shaolin novice tears up a lot of rice paper before finally being able to walk across it leaving no trace. At some point, however, the movement transcends the practice. The rules and structure fall away, along with the mover, and the movement flows effortlessly, perfectly, beautifully.

Because the sage is aligned with this concept, the sage's actions flow naturally, benefitting all beings impartially and compassionately, without regard to merit. This alignment is described as receiving insight, following the light, or, more poetically, cloaking oneself in enlightenment.

This is reflected in the mutuality of a teacher/student relationship. If properly aligned, the harmonious interdependence and interplay of this dynamic reflect the essence and mystery of Dao. We can appreciate this as we go through our day by considering everything and everyone we encounter to be our teacher. And we can recognize that we also bring something of value to the exchange.

When we approach life with a respectful, open attitude, without judgment or interference, we can experience and appreciate the vast wisdom that permeates all creation. We can cloak ourselves with enlightenment.

This is demonstrated in one of my favorite scenes in the *Kung Fu* TV series. The young novice encounters Master Po, who is blind. Master Po deftly teaches his student not to assume that just because he has no sight, he cannot be aware of his surroundings. He instructs the boy to close his eyes and listen, but the novice hears nothing.

Master Po: Can you hear the grasshopper at your feet?

Novice: Old man, how is it that you can hear these things?

Master Po: Young man, how is it that you cannot?

Chapter 28

Reconciling male and female
Become the watercourse for the world
Eternal De will never depart
Returning to innocence

Reconciling seen and unseen
Become a model for the world
Eternal De will never fail
Returning to limitlessness

Reconciling honor and humility
Become the valley of the world
Eternal De is thus fulfilled
Returning to wholeness

Wholeness disperses into form
The sage uses form in alignment
Thereby expending little energy
Like a master tailor who makes few cuts

Chapter 28 Reflections

The theme of this chapter is returning to our natural state. Dao is the undifferentiated source of the manifested universe. Dao manifests in the universe as De. De is loosely translated as virtue but does not mean virtue in the sense of morality, but rather in the sense of an inner harmony or natural integrity. De is not separate from Dao but rather is the natural expression or revelation of Dao in the world. De ultimately returns to its source in Dao.

When our own lives manifest the aligned integrity of De, we return to our natural state of harmony with Dao. This aligned integrity reconciles the illusion of opposites, recognizing the inherent mutuality of duality. The chapter provides three examples, reconciling male and female, seen and unseen, honor and humility. This reconciliation reveals the eternal dance of manifesting and returning. The energy of manifestation is described as ever present, never failing, completely fulfilled. The energy of returning is described as innocence, limitlessness, simplicity.

Nestled within this chapter are beautiful images that appear throughout the *Dao De Jing* to represent this interplay of mutuality.

The watercourse way is often used as a metaphor for the natural and effortless flow of creation. The innocence of infancy represents the primal unity of male and female, a pure channel through which De flows uninterrupted. Jesus spoke of the innocence of children and their closeness to the divine.

The image of a valley is also a theme. A valley is low, fertile, open. It lies humbly beneath the rolling hills or majestic mountains that surround it, providing shelter and quietly gathering the water that flows down from the heights, nourishing and sustaining all life that grows within its womb.

The character used for wholeness literally means an uncarved piece of wood, yet another theme. This conveys not only a meaning of simplicity but also of unlimited potential. An uncarved piece of wood contains infinite undifferentiated potential to become many things.

The images and poetry of this chapter reveal to us the rhythm of the universe, manifesting into form and returning to formlessness. Within that rhythm, we find the balance of duality, the still point around which duality circles in endless dance. When we surrender to the dance, we ourselves effortlessly become the watercourse way, the model of nature's perfection, the humble and fertile valley of all creation.

*O Lord, wilt thou not shut the gates of thy righteousness before me,
that I may walk in the path of the low valley,
that I may be strict in the plain road.*

~2 Nephi 4:32

Chapter 29

Efforts to interfere with the natural rhythm of the universe
Will not succeed
The world is a sacred vessel
That cannot be controlled or grasped
If you force it you will destroy it
If you grasp it you will lose it
Sometimes things are ahead, sometimes behind
Sometimes breath is gentle, sometimes hard
Sometimes strength is robust, sometimes weak
Sometimes energy expands, sometimes withdraws
Thus the sage avoids extremes
Leaving extravagance and arrogance behind

Chapter 29 Reflections

Our world is full of stories of efforts to improve something in our environment, efforts that lead to the need for further efforts to ameliorate unintended consequences. Interference becomes a self-perpetuating pattern.

We do the same thing with our "inner environment." The lucrative self-improvement industry thrives on our need to make ourselves better, smarter, prettier, more mindful, happier, more successful. It's exhausting and, like other misguided attempts to improve on nature, unending, as evidenced by one of my favorite book titles, *Death: The End of Self-Improvement*, by Joan Tollifson. There is nothing wrong, of course, with being happier or any of the other things listed, but when we start with the premise that we are deficient or unacceptable in some way, our efforts become a form of self-violence rather than self-care.

Like the world, we are a sacred vessel, created in harmony with a natural order that is whole and perfect. Our true nature is obscured by our self-judgment and our efforts to be something other than what we are. Our interference destroys our alignment and leaves us unbalanced, ever seeking what has always been ours.

What arrogance to think that we know best how things should be, how we should be. The character for arrogance 泰 depicts water slipping through the fingers of a hand, a fitting image for our futile efforts to hold on to and control the natural flow of energy through the universe and through our lives. Instead, like the sage, we can avoid extremes, choosing the middle path of balance and harmony. The middle path is the way of no way, not directing, not controlling, not judging, not dominating. It is the way of allowing, flowing, being present, responding appropriately. It manifests as kindness, simplicity, humility, joy, compassion, gratitude, peace.

When I am not at peace, chances are I am trying to control something I can't control, that I'm wanting reality to be something other than what it is, that I'm wanting myself to be something other than what I am. My efforts will fail, and in the process I will lose my awareness and experience of the beauty and sacred perfection of everything.

For peace of mind, resign as general manager of the universe.
  ~Larry Eisenberg

Chapter 30

One who lives in alignment with Dao
Does not use force to exert control
Force turns back upon itself
Briars grow where armies camp
War brings years of misery
Better to allow life to unfold as it will
Without presuming to know how things should be
Fruit grows naturally in harmony with the tree
Without boasting
Without judgment
Without arrogance
Without seeking advantage
Without striving or effort
What is not in harmony with Dao
Will soon exhaust itself

Chapter 30 Reflections

Some have characterized the theme of this chapter as karma, as in you reap what you sow. Sow goodness to reap goodness, but if you sow evil, evil will return to you. To me, however, this chapter carries forward from the last one the idea that sowing anything that interferes with the flow of energy in the universe will lead to disharmony and misfortune. The point, I think, is not that we shouldn't do good things, but rather that we should first root ourselves in Dao and allow the fruits of alignment to grow naturally. When our thoughts, words, and actions are attuned to the currents and vibrations of the universe, we don't do good as much as good happens through us. Everything remains in natural harmony and balance.

The chapter reminds us that force only begets force. When force is met with nonresistance, however, the force dissipates into nothingness or is turned back to its source. This was demonstrated to me once when I was practicing push hands (taiji sparring) with my teacher. He wanted to show me something he was working on, but it required me to push or advance toward him. I didn't know this, though, and I remained neutral, staying loose and ready.

In so doing, I unwittingly kept him from using his new technique. In fact, in his effort to force the maneuver, he got a bit off balance himself. When he complimented me on uprooting him, I realized that I really had done nothing; he had uprooted himself. Our encounter taught me a valuable lesson, not only in martial arts but also in life.

The character for fruit 果, showing a field resting on top of a tree, is used in this chapter six times. It also means results, resolution, achieving a purpose. The image encourages us to focus on alignment in the way a tree is rooted in the earth with its needs met for sun and water. When conditions are in harmony, fruit naturally manifests on a healthy tree like a field yielding a bountiful harvest. There is no need for force or effort, which would only bring exhaustion. Nor does the tree need to boast or take credit for what it produces. Everything just happens in accordance with its nature.

This same concept is described in the Bible, where alignment with God allows the Holy Spirit to manifest through us as "fruits of the spirit," such as kindness, joy, peace, generosity. It's a natural process, in contrast to externally imposed rules of correct behavior, which often leave us feeling drained by our efforts to comply and frustrated by our perceived shortcomings. Life invites us to join in the mystical, cosmic dance of existence, to root ourselves in beauty, be showered with grace, and allow ourselves to bloom.

By their fruits ye shall know them.

~Matthew 7:16

Chapter 31

Even excellent weapons are inauspicious
Creatures instinctively shun them
Those aligned with Dao do not rely on them
The wise ruler faces east
While soldiers march in the west
Using weapons only as a last resort
The ruler takes no pleasure in battle
Preferring peace to war
Rejoicing not in winning
Mourning all whose lives are lost
Those who thirst for blood
Will never be satisfied in this world
Or understand the victor's sorrow in success

Chapter 31 Reflections

As a contracts lawyer, I always entered negotiations with a goal of reaching an agreement that both parties considered a win. Starting with an adversarial attitude, even when my client had the superior bargaining position, rarely let to harmonious business relations.

When I consider arguments I've engaged in, it's hard to find even one that left me feeling good about fighting. Even if I got the desired outcome, I paid a price, perhaps causing damage to a relationship, hurting someone unnecessarily, or just feeling my energy drained. There was rarely lasting pleasure in victory. That might sound odd coming from someone who enjoys practicing with martial arts weapons. Contradictory as it seems, engaging in martial arts over the years has taught me more about peace than about fighting. Learning how to de-escalate and redirect energy to avoid direct confrontation has served me well in martial arts and even better in life.

This chapter invites us to explore the nature of conflict. What conditions create an experience of conflict and how do we respond to it? Conflict is rooted in judgment. Something is good or bad; someone is right or wrong. Connection gives way to separation, which in turn gives way to opposition and the anticipation of a win/lose outcome. And no one wants to be the loser. Opportunities to connect and foster relationship to resolve issues are lost in the scramble to gain the upper hand and press home an advantage.

This is just as true in the context of internal conflict, when we become our own worst enemy full of self-condemnation rather than self-compassion, forcing ourselves in a particular direction rather than listening to the inner wisdom of our heart.

If we trace the development of any external or internal conflict back to its origin, we might find that there is a moment before separation occurs, when the situation has not yet been identified or experienced as adversarial. In that moment is tremendous power, the power to choose. And there is really only one choice being made, between fear and love. If we can pause in that moment and acknowledge the fear, we can embrace it with compassion rather than react to it. We can understand the fear without letting it dictate our response. We can remain whole rather than fragmenting into opposing sides.

Even if taking a stand is called for, we can do what is needed without rejecting or closing our hearts to ourselves or others. We can choose love even on the battlefield.

A house divided against itself cannot stand.
~Mark 3:25, quoted by Abraham Lincoln

Chapter 32

Dao is forever beyond names
Though by nature simple and humble
Nothing under heaven can rule over it
If princes and kings aligned with it
The ten thousand things would be honored like guests
When heaven and earth join together
Blessings fall like sweet dew
People live in harmony
To impose order rules are named
Rules lead to more rules
Knowing when to stop avoids harm
Dao's way under heaven
Is like a river flowing through the valley to the sea

Chapter 32 Reflections

This chapter picks up the relationship first described in Chapter 1 between the nameless and the named. Dao is beyond names, beyond identification or limitation. It is the undifferentiated, formless, infinite potential of Dao from which emerge the ten thousand things of form. Each form has a name. It becomes this and not that. This limitation is not a bad thing. After all, Michelangelo created from uncarved blocks of marble timeless forms of beauty.

Naming is powerful. When aligned with the nameless source of Dao, naming creates a natural synergy of dynamic energy between the formless and the formed. The reference to rulers of government can apply just as well to our own internal guidance. When we are attuned to this dynamic energy, everything moves in harmony without the need for external enforcement. But when we are out of alignment, we start to impose an artificial structure of "named" rules. We see this in our own lives and in our systems of law and government, where rules beget more rules ad infinitum.

I'm not opposed to rules. I certainly had a few rules in my own household that brought moments of stability out of the chaos of so many kids. But I also knew there was a tipping point beyond which too many rules were counterproductive. As always, there is a middle road of balance and a sense of ease when we align ourselves with the natural order of the universe.

This natural order has rules too. The river flowing through the valley to the sea follows the law of gravity as it shapes and is shaped by the channels through which it runs. Thus aligned, it flows freely, effortlessly, in harmony with all creation, connected always to the source from which it comes and to which it will return.

This chapter invites us to consider the rules we have adopted in our own lives. Do they foster or block the natural flow of energy in our lives? Do they support us or exhaust us? Do they connect us to a sense of oneness or isolate us from the sea of common existence?

I would love to live like a river flows, carried by the surprise of its own unfolding.

~John O'Donohue

Chapter 33

Knowing others is wisdom
Knowing the self is enlightenment
Conquering others requires force
Conquering the self requires inner strength
Living in contentment is true abundance
Living in alignment is true mastery
One who stays centered endures
What is immortal never dies

Chapter 33 Reflections

Our deepest fear is not that we are inadequate. Our deepest fear is that we are powerful beyond measure.

~Marianne Williamson

This chapter is about power, not power over someone or something, but power within. "Power over" is individual and measurable; one side is stronger than another and exerts that force to control or gain some advantage. "Power within" is universal and unlimited; it is the intrinsic power of existence. It is Shakti, the life energy within all creation, including within us. One of us doesn't have more of it than any other. We don't have to seek it, find it, generate it, gather it, hoard it, or cultivate it. We can't not have it. We *are* it.

The chapter tells us that knowing others is wisdom, but knowing the self is enlightenment. "Know thyself," counsels the inscription above the door to Apollo's temple where the Oracle of Delphi resides. Apollo is the Greek sun god, and it's no coincidence, I think, that the Chinese character for sun 日 appears in the characters for wisdom 智 (on the bottom) and enlightenment 明 (on the left). If knowledge is power, as the saying goes, then this is powerful knowledge indeed, the infinite power of awakened awareness.

So why would being "powerful beyond measure" be our deepest fear? It can be scary because we've forgotten who we are. When we see ourselves as separate and alone, such power can feel overwhelming. But when we awaken to remember that we are all part of the universal web of being, always and forever connected to the origin of creation, that power is liberated within us to move freely through our lives. When we are aligned, our own energy vibrates in harmony with universal energy, because they are one and the same. We manifest true mastery.

The character for mastery 志 places the symbol for warrior over the symbol for heart. As awakened beings, we become fearless warriors of the heart, shining the light of love on all we see, just as the sun shines on all the earth and radiates light into the galaxy and beyond. We are content, and all is well.

Question: In all the universe is there one single thing of value?

Answer: Yes, the power of love.

~Nisargadatta Maharaj, *I Am That*

Chapter 34

Great Dao flows everywhere left and right
The ten thousand things depend on it
It gives birth to all and refuses none
It accomplishes without acclaim
Nourishing the ten thousand things without ruling
Without desire it remains small
Yet the ten thousand things return home to it
Thus it is very great
Because it seeks no greatness
It is truly great

Chapter 34 Reflections

This sweet little chapter portrays the relationship between Dao and the manifested universe. It begins with another water image for Dao. Water is the metaphor most often used to represent the nature of Dao. The character 汜, meaning flow, has the water radical on the left (the three slanted lines). The right side means to spring forth, so there is a sense here of water welling up and overflowing, giving life and nourishment to all existence.

Throughout this chapter Dao is described as unassuming, small, fulfilling its role without claiming credit or lording it over creation. And yet its greatness is emphasized multiple times. The character for greatness 大 looks like a person standing with arms outstretched, welcoming, embracing all the ten thousand things without exception or reservation. Dao remains unchanging, infinite, formless, eternal, the source from which the manifested universe emerges and to which it returns in the ever-repeating cycle of life, like a wave that washes up on the shore, but is never separated from the sea to which it returns. So generous. So loving.

Dao achieves its great purpose naturally, effortlessly, without agenda or judgment. Have you ever been amazed at something you easily accomplished and wondered, "How did that happen?" Perhaps it seemed like you were just present while marvels unfolded all around you and through you. To me, that is what this chapter describes. When we surrender our own agenda and our own need for recognition, the true power of the universe moves all around us and through us. And miracles happen.

When Love crashes through mind's familiar understanding of how things ought to be, mind can only cry out, "That's a miracle!" "No," Love answers, "that's just the way I am."

~Emmanuel's Book III

Chapter 35

Adhere to the natural order of the universe
Followed by everything under heaven
Alignment protects from harm
Bringing peace, harmony, abundance
Music and fine food lure passersby to stop
But Dao moves unnoticed
Taste – it is without flavor
Look – it is without form
Listen – it is without sound
Yet its blessings never cease

Chapter 35 Reflections

This timeless chapter could have been written today instead of 2500 years ago. It reminds us that what has true and lasting value is often overlooked in the hubbub of a busy world seeking ever more loud and glittering distraction. A cultural mantra of "more, more, more," leaves us feeling less and less content.

Always searching for greater sensory stimulation obscures the subtle rhythm and beauty of Dao. It is not found out there, but in here, in the silence of our souls. We find it not by seeking, but by allowing. When we pause our efforts to do more and be better, our body, mind, and spirit will effortlessly settle into resonance with the vibration of all creation. This alignment brings peace, harmony, and abundance into our lives, not as a result of our striving, but as an expression of the inherent perfection of the natural order of the universe.

Our culture is geared towards going after what we want, setting goals and achieving them, earning our rewards, seeking sensory entertainment, and competing to be best. The notion of appreciating things as they are, accepting our place in the great order, and simply receiving the bounty of creation, may seem incomprehensible. And yet, this is exactly what the *Dao De Jing* counsels us to do.

Even if we accept the concept of inner harmony as desirable, we might still feel flummoxed as to how to access this state of contentment. How do we move from the idea to the experience of natural alignment and the blessings that it brings?

The character for natural order 象 has many meanings, including image, icon, majestic, phenomenon, form…and elephant! When combined with the character for great, as it is in the first line of this chapter 大 象, it means the "great order," the unifying patterns that regulate and harmonize all phenomena in the manifested universe. That's impressive. But I keep coming back to that elephant. What is it about elephants that would represent the grand scheme of creation? These juxtapositions of meanings in Chinese characters invite us to consider their possible significance. Is there something about elephants that might guide us into alignment?

What comes to mind first is that despite their overwhelming size, elephants are incredibly gentle and sensitive. They are mindful in their actions. They are led by the yin energy of the matriarch. They feel vibrations through the earth and communicate through sounds below our hearing range. And they are emotionally connected and devoted to each other. I'm sure there's more, but perhaps this quote sums it up best.

Nature's great masterpiece, an elephant; the only harmless great thing.
~John Donne

Chapter 36

If one wants to draw in
  One must first expand
If one wants to weaken
  One must first strengthen
If one wants to discard
  One must first raise up
If one wants to receive
  One must first give
This is the mystery of enlightenment

Chapter 36 Reflections

This chapter repeats a theme in the *Dao De Jing* of the interdependence and creative energy of what some think of as opposites but are really balancing or complementary energies. My taiji teacher is fond of saying, "If something goes up, something comes down." This is how he explains the exchange of energy between yin and yang. If one is filling, the other is emptying. We draw in to manifest out. We yield to overcome force.

This relationship of unity and harmony between these energies reveals the illusion of conflict. I have found this to be true in many situations where an escalating argument is easily flipped around by finding a way to connect on common ground. I once watched two parents disagree about whether their water-averse child should take swimming lessons. Instead of tempers rising in a rigid win/lose position, they realized that they both loved their child and wanted their child to be comfortable in the water. They agreed on an approach that addressed both their concerns. There never was any actual conflict. And really, there never is.

Understanding this illusion of conflict between interrelated energies is called the mystery of enlightenment. The character for mystery also means subtle, intangible, hidden. It describes the thin place between the emptiness of Dao and the manifestation of the ten thousand things, the liminal space between form and formlessness. At this point of intersection, the energy of what appears as two opposites swirls together, generating the creative power of the universe.

The "magic" of this creative power is nowhere more evident than in the realm of the heart. When we think in finite terms of distinctions and limitations, it is obvious that if I give you something I have less. But in the heart realm, giving begins the dance of creation as the two sides of giving and receiving join to give birth to more than the sum of the parts. This is not something to analyze; we grasp its truth in experience.

Once when I was so depleted by circumstances in my life, all I could think of was that I needed help. Somehow, as counterintuitive as it seemed, I entered a training program to help others. Although I couldn't imagine having enough inner resources to be of any use to anyone, I was amazed to find that I drew strength and healing from giving to others what I needed for myself. Magic indeed.

My bounty is as boundless as the sea, my love as deep. The more I give to thee, the more I have, for both are infinite.

~Shakespeare, *Romeo and Juliet*

Chapter 37

Eternal Dao remains still
Yet all is accomplished
If princes and kings are aligned with it
The ten thousand things will naturally transform
Any arousing desire will be quieted by nameless simplicity
Without desire there is tranquility
Everything under heaven is naturally in harmony

Chapter 37 Reflections

The opening couplet in this chapter shows up several times in the *Dao De Jing*. The characters literally mean Dao always without acting, yet without not acting. This is often translated as Dao does nothing, yet nothing is left undone. The concept of nonaction or *wu wei* causes much confusion when interpreted as static passivity. But it makes sense when understood as harmony with the basic order and nature of the universe. When aligned with this energy, things happen and unfold naturally, without striving or exerting force or imposing control. In that way, all that needs to happen is accomplished, and nothing unnecessary interferes.

Heroic actions are often manifestations of this dynamic power. Ordinary people who do extraordinary things in a crisis sometimes describe what they did as happening spontaneously without giving any thought to it. Athletes and artists describe being in the zone, in which their performance seems to be manifesting through them rather than from them. And yes, sometimes this harmony appears as stillness when action would be interfering with the natural order.

The *Dao De Jing* makes many references to rulers or ruling. These passages could apply to actual government but could also be referring to how we govern ourselves. If we abide by the natural order of Dao, we are awakened to our innate harmony with all creation. The struggle we experience when we desire things to be other than what they are, or desire ourselves to be other than what we are, is quieted by Dao's natural simplicity, which is universal and beyond description.

The link between desire and suffering is part of Buddhism's Four Noble Truths. I can see this in my own life when I try to assert control to make things conform to how I want them to be. I am not tranquil. I suffer. I instinctively know, whether I consciously recognize it, that I am not in harmony with Dao's natural rhythm. I might describe my discomfort as being out of sync, not in tune, out of sorts. When I return to alignment, there is a sigh of relief. Even if there is a lot happening around me, I am at peace.

The character used here for harmony 定 has a top part that means roof and a bottom part that means upright or correct. So there is a sense of being sheltered or protected by correct alignment. When we are in alignment with Dao, we need not be concerned about anything. Life unfolds as it should and carries us on its currents. We can be at peace and enjoy the ride.

Peace I leave with you; my peace I give you. I do not give to you as the world gives. Do not let your hearts be troubled and do not be afraid.

~John 14:27

Chapter 38

True De is not contrived
And thus is naturally virtuous
Contrived virtue is imposed
And thus is without harmony
True De is effortless
Yet all unfolds perfectly
Contrived virtue is intentional
Yet struggles to achieve order
Kindness acts selflessly towards all
While justice seeks to remedy a wrong
Propriety requires compliance
And when ignored resorts to force
Thus when Dao is lost De arises
When De is lost kindness arises
When kindness is lost justice arises
When justice is lost propriety arises
Propriety falls far from the heart's true center
Chaos and confusion follow closely on its heels
In ignorance of Dao's perfection folly reigns
Thus the wise abide in substance and not in appearance
They abide in the fruit and not in the flower
They leave the trappings and choose the essence

Chapter 38 Reflections

This chapter contains one of my favorite passages in the *Dao De Jing*, outlining a hierarchy of qualities, each one arising as the former one is lost.

When looking at the Chinese characters for this progression of qualities, I noticed that the concept of an individual "I" does not appear until the character for justice. Until that point, the character components for Dao, De, and kindness suggest unity and connection. But when we get to the character for justice, we lose that sense of interrelatedness. The focus shifts to the individual with a component that means "I" or first person.

When I taught law, I had my students read this passage on the first day of class. Justice is one of our highest ideals, and as lawyers we vow to seek it and uphold it. However, as I pointed out to my students, look how far down the list justice falls. Justice rises to the top as a guiding principle only after we have lost our natural alignment with Dao and De, and our heart connection to others through kindness. Justice is the last stand of society before the empty ritual of propriety gives way to chaos and confusion.

That doesn't make justice bad. As a member of the legal profession and as an individual, I honor my commitment to justice. I'm reminded of the Bible's urging to do justice, love kindness, and walk humbly with our God.

The issue, perhaps, is one of priorities, as the hierarchy in the chapter suggests. Steven Covey says that "the main thing is to keep the main thing the main thing." If my focus is on living in harmony with Dao, then everything else in the hierarchy naturally manifests. I wouldn't have to seek justice because injustice would never occur. I wouldn't need to cultivate kindness because kindness would be my natural expression. I could walk no other way than humbly, because I would know myself as part of something far greater than my individual ego.

I sometimes feel frustrated or discouraged when I look at the world. When I am in a certain frame of mind, it appears that indeed we have fallen all the way down the list into chaos and confusion. People fight over rules, shouting justice, when it seems evident, at least on some days, that there is no guidance being sought from further up the list.

But, as the saying goes, as within so without. We need look no further than our own lives – our own thoughts, words, and actions – and consider where in the hierarchy our own guidance falls. Sometimes it might seem far down the list. At those times, especially when we feel stuck, perhaps we can turn the light of kindness towards our own hearts, accepting ourselves as we are in that moment.

The scales of justice are not balanced by judging the wrong and praising the right, but from letting go of all illusions.

~James Blanchard Cisneros

Chapter 39

From ancient times all creation reflects oneness
In oneness:
Heaven is clear
Earth is serene
The soul is divine
Valleys are abundant
The ten thousand things are born
Rulers are virtuous
And oneness connects them all

Otherwise:
Heaven without clarity would split open
Earth without serenity would collapse
The soul without divinity would wither away
The valley without abundance would be exhausted
The ten thousand things without birth would disappear
Rulers without virtue would falter

Honor is rooted in humility
Low is the foundation of the high
Therefore embrace humility as your foundation
Do not shine like jade
Or clatter like stones

Chapter 39 Reflections

Dao and the ten thousand things – formless oneness manifesting in countless forms, all interconnected and in harmony with the one. It's like invisible light refracting through a prism into the differentiated colors of the rainbow. The differentiation makes light visible, but the one and the many are all the same light. Similarly, the ten thousand things are never separated from each other or from their source.

The chapter first describes the qualities of various aspects of creation aligned and in harmony with oneness. The second part mirrors the first and describes the result of losing connection with oneness.

This invites us to consider our own lives. When we are aligned and in harmony with the universe, everything is as it should be – effortless, peaceful, energized, abundant. When we experience ourselves as part of the infinite oneness of the universe, we are part of something much more vast, more beautiful, more perfect, than our individual egos could ever imagine or attain. In contrast, when we see ourselves as separate individuals, unconnected to each other and to the source from which we all emerge, we believe that we have to be in control of everything. That is a terrifying responsibility, and an impossible one to meet. In our futile efforts we are exhausted, driven by anxiety and self-judgment because we never measure up.

How do we stay in alignment? The last part of the chapter counsels us to embrace humility as our foundation. From this foundation, we are able to allow the power of the universe to move through us, guiding us, carrying us, protecting us, loving us. We are one with all creation, trusting the perfection of the grand design beyond our comprehension. We need not force circumstances or control events. Our responsibility is to listen and allow. What is ours to do is clear and we are well able to do what is called for. We rest in the awareness that we are never alone or abandoned, knowing that the entire universe embraces us with love, because the entire universe *is* love, and we are that.

> *You are not limited to this body, to this mind, or to this reality—you are a limitless ocean of Consciousness, imbued with infinite potential. You are existence itself.*
>
> ~Joseph P. Kauffman

Chapter 40

Returning is Dao's motion
Through supple tenderness
All under heaven is born from being
Being is born from nonbeing

Chapter 40 Reflections

This lovely little four-line chapter has been described as the *Dao De Jing's* theology in a nutshell. That always makes me smile. The *Dao De Jing* is so simple in its philosophy, like the uncarved piece of wood often used as a metaphor, transcendent in its beauty and truth, like a timeless piece of music or art, and practical in its application, like a how-to manual for living in alignment.

The first line describes the cyclic energy of creation. The ten thousand things of the manifested universe endlessly return to their source in the formless void of Dao. The creative energy of Dao then returns to form as it ceaselessly generates and produces the ten thousand things. Form and formlessness, being and nonbeing, the named and the nameless, life and death, unity and relationship, in an eternal dance of tender exchange. So beautiful.

And as near to us as our breath. With each breath we live the creative, returning motion of Dao. Life breathes us into being and we release into nonbeing with every inhale and exhale. It happens naturally, effortlessly, without any interference on our part. We don't need to learn how to do it, or to understand the mechanics of it. Let your breath be your guru, teaching you everything you need to know about existence, bringing you into the present moment with the breath you are breathing as you read these words. This is it, all there is. Perfect.

The Tantric sages tell us that our in-breath and out-breath actually mirror the divine creative gesture.

~Sally Kempton

Chapter 41

The high scholar hears Dao and diligently practices it
The middle scholar hears Dao and sometimes remembers it,
    sometimes forgets it
The low scholar hears Dao and has a great laugh
Without laughter one cannot follow Dao
Thus it is said:
Bright Dao seems dark
Dao going forward seems to retreat
Level Dao seems uneven
High De seems like a valley
Great purity seems sullied
Abundant De seems insufficient
Upright De seems unsteady
Genuine truth seems uncertain
Great place has no boundaries
Great vessel is slow to fill
Great sound is silent
Great form has no shape
Dao is hidden without name
Truly Dao's goodness is generous and complete

Chapter 41 Reflections

I love this chapter because its opening passage reveals a lot about the reader. I always loved school, and I was a diligent student, so I can relate to the high scholar of Dao. Indeed, many commentators place more value on being the diligent high scholar than on the middle or low scholar. "High" and "low" are sometimes translated in this chapter as "superior" and "inferior," lending further support to this interpretation.

However, I came to question the assumption that we should strive to practice Dao diligently like the high scholar. Nowhere else in the *Dao De Jing* are we encouraged to make such effort. On the contrary, we are taught that the path of harmony with Dao is not to learn but to unlearn, not to practice diligently but to flow effortlessly. Perhaps we have missed the point in these opening lines by so quickly admiring the high scholar. The low scholar hears Dao and laughs. This seems more in keeping with other descriptions of the sage as innocent like a child, without ambition, acting without effort, even appearing foolish to others. I'm reminded of the Dalai Lama who laughs easily and often, and never seems to take himself too seriously.

The lines that follow this opening passage suggest that things are not always what they appear to be. In the same way, the high achievement of the diligent scholar is not necessarily in harmony with Dao. And what we might dismiss as the fool's laughter could really be the sage's deep awareness of Dao's essence. This chapter invites us to consider our relationship with Dao. Rather than something difficult to be mastered, perhaps it is something natural to be enjoyed. My quick identification with the high scholar has given me a great laugh...at myself!

If you find it hard to laugh at yourself, I would be happy to do it for you.
~Groucho Marx

Chapter 42

Dao gives birth to one
One gives birth to two
Two give birth to three
Three give birth to the ten thousand things
The ten thousand things carry yin and embrace yang
Merging the energy of both to create harmony
People reject orphans and widows
But kings and lords embrace the lowly
Sometimes there is loss and sometimes gain
Sometimes benefit and sometimes suffering
What people manifest will return to them
As we live so will we die
I hold this teaching as my guide

Chapter 42 Reflections

If Chapter 40 presents the *Dao De Jing's* theology in a nutshell, the first four lines of this chapter present its creation story in a nutshell. Using symbols, this progression can be illustrated by the movement from wuji to taiji.

The wuji symbol is an open circle, representing the undifferentiated, limitless potential of Dao. The circle is open to indicate the limitless expanse of infinity. The symbol for taiji is the yin yang symbol, showing the dark yin and the light yang halves ever transforming one into the other. The union of yin and yang ultimately produce the ten thousand things of the manifested universe, which, as the chapter tells us, carry yin and embrace yang. The character for carry 负 suggests carrying yin on one's back, while yang is embraced 抱 in the front, giving us a sense of yin and yang circulating through us and around us in perfect balance, one fading as the other manifests, merging their energies to create harmony.

We see this in the impermanence of circumstances, gain and loss, benefit and suffering. And of course, in the rhythm of our breathing. There is a moment between an inhale and exhale, a moment of balanced stillness as the two energies meet in the center before exchanging places and repeating the cycle. Within that stillness is perfect, eternal harmony. In Shambhala training, this point between the breaths is called the gap. It is the gateway of the holy instant described in *A Course in Miracles*. Within that tiny portal is the transcendence of time into the vastness of infinity, the return to the formless emptiness of wuji before separating again into the dual energies of yin and yang.

A visiting law professor once gave us an instruction to turn to a particular page in our book and "be amazed." That might have been my favorite instruction in law school. Our breath is like that. It seems ordinary and we take it for granted. But within each breath is all the wisdom teaching of the universe. Be amazed.

There are no words in silence
Words create two
When I speak, I speak to God
Who else is there

~Galen Pearl

Chapter 43

What is most soft
Overcomes what is most hard
What is without form
Can enter the impenetrable
By this I understand wu wei's benefit
Teaching without words
Abundance without effort
Few under heaven attain this

Chapter 43 Reflections

Again we see here the advantage of yielding, allowing, being like water. Water is soft but overcomes even solid rock. I am delighted by the two characters used to mean overcome, which literally mean to gallop on horseback. This brings back wonderful childhood memories of galloping bareback across meadows, hands entwined in flowing mane, hanging on as my horse ran free. It was exhilarating and powerful. The horse's strength came from being supple, its speed from finding its rhythm. What a poetic image of softness overcoming rigidity.

The image of the formless penetrating everywhere evokes a different memory of being inadvertently caught in a revolution in another country. With just minutes of warning, some fellow travelers and I crowded into a hotel room as tear gas canisters exploded in the street below. Although we quickly stuffed wet towels around windows hoping to seal them, within moments our eyes were red and stinging, vividly demonstrating the truth of this passage.

Much of what I practice in martial arts is about not being stiff or forceful. As one teacher says, "I know you, but you do not know me." He means that he can sense where our resistance is, whereas he remains fluid and elusive. If I push, I meet nothing and suddenly my effort is my own defeat. "I'm trying...," I begin. "That's your problem," he laughs in response.

Just like in life. I've learned from my grandchildren something I never mastered with my strong-willed children. Don't meet force with force, but rather overcome with softness. It's amazing how much easier it is to deflect or redirect energy by moving with it rather than meeting it head on. We exhaust ourselves with our force and resistance, trying to make circumstances or people something other than what they are. But each new moment gives us another chance to mount up and gallop over whatever obstacles we meet.

Galloping is trust and honesty between horse and rider and pure, amazing energy.

~Ella West

Chapter 44

Status or integrity, which is dearer
Integrity or wealth, which is greater
Gain or loss, which is more painful
Excessive attachment comes at great cost
Acquiring more and more brings great loss
Knowing contentment avoids dishonor
Knowing when to stop avoids trouble
In this way one remains at peace

Chapter 44 Reflections

The first two lines remind me of the popular question: Would you rather be rich or famous? Here, however, we are invited to evaluate both status and riches in comparison to our self. The character for integrity 身 originally meant pregnant and depicted a woman carrying a child in her womb, but over time the meaning expanded to include our physical body, our sense of self or identity, and also integrity. So the concept of self in this chapter does not mean self-centered or selfish, but rather our very being, infused with life force, integrated and whole. Status and riches would not seem to stack up very well in comparison, and yet how many people sacrifice everything to attain them?

To what end? The external things we chase after and try to hold on to do not bring us the happiness we anticipate. Fame comes and goes. Riches often create dissatisfaction as we fear to lose what we have and relentlessly seek, as billionaire J. D. Rockefeller said, "just a little more." The message here is one of balance and equanimity. We receive and release. There is a point of equipoise where we remain balanced, not seeking to force or interfere.

Sometimes people misinterpret this to mean that we should sit around doing nothing. That is not in harmony. When it is time to work, we work. When it is time to rest, we rest. We take responsibility for our lives. We provide for our families. We contribute to our communities. We can do all that from a centered place of contentment and gratitude, knowing when we have enough or have done enough.

My sister is an artist, and I often wonder how she knows that a painting is finished. There seems to be a point at which she has done enough, and more would be too much. When I ask her how she knows, she shrugs, "I just know." That fascinates me.

On the other hand, I have a friend who lives in a palatial home but is chronically stressed about money. How can a person who lives in such luxury have such a joy-crushing sense of lack? That also fascinates me.

This chapter invites us to examine our own lives, to notice where we struggle to maintain the scales in an out-of-balance position. Consider the effort it takes to sustain that disequilibrium. If we can explore this with curiosity and without self-judgment, perhaps we can gain some insight and release just a little of the burden that we place on our own shoulders. We can take a deep breath, restore balance, and be at peace.

Be cool at the equator; keep thy blood fluid at the Pole.
~Herman Melville, *Moby Dick*

Chapter 45

Great perfection seems flawed
But its use is not impaired
Great abundance seems empty
Yet its use is not exhausted
Great justice seems wrong
Great skill seems clumsy
Great eloquence seems awkward
Great riches seem poor
Movement overcomes cold
Stillness overcomes heat
Clarity and tranquility align everything under heaven

Chapter 45 Reflections

The Chinese character for "seems" is used repeatedly in this chapter, suggesting that perhaps things are not always as they appear, or not always what we think them to be. I'm reminded of 1 Corinthians 13:12: "For now we see through a glass darkly, but then face to face." Or, as Anaïs Nin said, "We don't see things as they are; we see them as we are."

We think we see clearly, but when we look through the glass of our perception, it is clouded by our own judgments and beliefs, our hopes and fears, and our opinions about how we think things should be or how we want them to be. We see illusion yet think it real. We see our own perceptions and label them as fact. We try to generalize our personal viewpoint and insist that it is universal. We seek the safety of certainty instead of the mystery of truth.

Our brains are wired to label, categorize, and organize information and experience. They are so determined in their quest to create a stable mental structure that they obscure our direct and immediate apprehension of what is with a quick explanation drawn from memory files. Just because we think it doesn't make it true. As the song title cautions, "It Ain't Necessarily So."

This chapter invites us to be aware of the lens through which we view the world, to question the assumptions that we hold as fact, to open our minds to create space for true knowing to unfurl and blossom. In martial arts we practice wuji stance, or empty stance. From this perfectly aligned, relaxed stance, we are balanced, in harmony with all that is, within and without. From this stance, all movement is possible, the internal circulation of energy is unrestricted, and the potential for outward expression of power is unlimited.

We can cultivate this same "stance" in our lives by finding our inner balance and alignment. When we are fully present with an attitude of open awareness, we engage with life as it truly is, as we truly are. We see face to face.

Every object, every creature, every man, woman, and child
has a soul,
and it is the destiny of all
to see as God sees,
to know as God knows,
to feel as God feels,
to Be
as God
Is

~Meister Eckhart

Chapter 46

When the world is aligned with Dao
Horses work in the fields
When the world is not aligned with Dao
War horses are bred outside the city
There is no greater punishment than having desire
There is no greater curse than obtaining your desire
There is no greater tribulation than not knowing contentment
Those who know contentment will always be satisfied

Chapter 46 Reflections

This chapter contrasts discontent and satisfaction. It begins with vivid imagery comparing horses working in the field to horses bred for war. Horses working in the field suggest times of peace and the abundance of harvest. War horses are associated with conflict and devastation. Life and death.

These are images of external peace and conflict, but we can also think in terms of whether we have peace or war inside of us. Whatever we have within is the energy we will offer to the world. Many of us look around at the turmoil in the world and want to help. But our way of helping contributes to dissension if our words and actions convey judgment and coercion. Even if our words speak of peace, if there is internal struggle, what we transmit is conflict. As the saying goes, as within so without.

Internal struggle is always rooted in desire, wanting something or someone (including ourselves) to be different, wanting reality to be different. Reality might be pleasurable or painful, and painful circumstances can certainly bring suffering. But we add to our suffering by our unwillingness to acknowledge reality as it is, by our grasping to hold on to fleeting pleasure or our aversion to what we dislike or reject.

Even getting what we desire can be a curse. When we get what we desire, it sometimes isn't what we thought it would be and we are disappointed. Or if it is exactly what we want or even better, it isn't long before we want more or something else. We think our dissatisfaction comes from not having what we want, but perhaps our dissatisfaction comes from wanting.

The character for contentment 足 also means satisfaction, sufficient, enough. It literally means foot and sort of looks like a person walking forward. When we stand with our feet on the ground, stable, rooted, centered, we need nothing. We have everything necessary to be where we are, because where we are is the only place we can be. It is enough.

Content makes poor men rich; discontent makes rich men poor.
~Benjamin Franklin

Chapter 47

Not leaving through the door
Know everything under heaven
Not looking through the window
Perceive heaven's Dao
The further one goes
The less one knows
Thus the sage travels not, yet knows
Seeks not, yet understands
Strives not, yet fulfills

Chapter 47 Reflections

This short chapter makes clear that we need not look anywhere outside ourselves for the answers we seek. In fact, we need not look at all.

We read of cloistered mystics, of wise hermits living in caves. Dorothy in *The Wizard of Oz* learned after an adventurous quest that everything she wanted was in her own backyard, where it had been all along. My Aunt Bernice never strayed far from home yet understood more about life than most people with more education and worldly experience. How did all these folks gain such wisdom?

We could take this chapter literally, cancel our vacation plans and let our passports expire. However, I don't think the caution here is against travel per se, but against looking outside of ourselves to find truth. To go even farther (pun intended), perhaps it is the very concept of seeking, whether out there or within, that frustrates our aspirations of awakening.

Many people describe themselves as seekers, content to always be searching for what they assume will always be beyond their reach. I used to joke that I didn't want to be a seeker; I wanted to be a finder! But seeking or finding suggests that there is something I want that I don't already have. What if what we are seeking can't be found because it was never lost?

We might embrace the idea that what we seek isn't out there, but within. However, we then continue the same search, just in a different direction. *Oh, it's within me! Where is it?* We search the inner terrain with the same determination as we searched the world over. *It's right here, I know it. I just need to meditate more (chant, pray, beat drums, walk labyrinths, read more books, do yoga). I know it's close. But I can't see it. Damn.* We're like the child who covers her eyes with her hands and says, "I can't see!" We don't need to find the light; we just need to remove what blocks our vision of the light that is all around us.

What happens if we quit searching? What happens if we just live fully in the present moment? And in this one? We know everything under heaven. We perceive heaven's *Dao*. It looks just like life. And it's marvelous.

> *Nor will people say, "Look, here it is," or "There it is." For you see, the kingdom of God is within you.*
>
> ~Luke 17:21

Chapter 48

Engaged in learning
We acquire every day
Engaged with Dao
We release every day
Release and again release
Until we have released everything
Then all unfolds effortlessly
Striving only interferes with this unfolding
It will never be enough to control Heaven's way

Chapter 48 Reflections

The first lines of this chapter caught my attention because I love to learn things, so acquiring more knowledge about whatever I'm interested in is always appealing. We might think that the opening lines portray a dim view of learning, but this should be taken in context. The *Dao De Jing* presented in its day, and still does present, an approach to life that is less about how to make ourselves and the world conform to how we think things should be, and more about an effortless and more intuitive alignment with the natural flow of energy in the universe. The text offers an alternative to the rigidly structured society envisioned by Confucius, occasionally taking issue with the Confucian emphasis on the superiority of the well-educated man.

So while I do enjoy learning, I understand that no amount of information will provide access to what is beyond the mind's capacity to grasp. To go beyond is to release everything we think we know, and to enter the infinite mystery of existence. As wisdom teachers have said, you can't think your way to truth. This is a challenging concept for our brains, which are wired to analyze, categorize, and evaluate. What is the secret of this apparent paradox? How do we convince our busy brains that when we cease striving with our exhausting efforts, when we release our urge to interfere and our compulsion to control, somehow everything will be okay?

This requires trust. The *Dao De Jing* envisions a universe that is self-regulating, with a rhythm and harmony that is inherent in creation. This is the opposite of a perspective that suggests that we can and should improve on nature. In our over-scheduled, never-enough-time, always-behind world, it seems crazy to think that doing less will accomplish more. Perhaps we might discover that less really needed to be accomplished in the first place. Either way, life seems more spacious, more delightful, more balanced than when we are struggling to acquire more, do more, be more. And in that spaciousness, our consciousness expands beyond the mind to reveal the exquisite perfection of what has been there all along.

Gate, gate, para gate, parasam gate, bodhi svaha (Gone, gone, gone beyond, gone completely beyond, enlightenment amen)

~mantra at the end of the *Heart Sutra*

Chapter 49

I am good to those who are good
I am good to those who are not good
De is goodness
I am trustworthy to those who are trustworthy
I am trustworthy to those who are not trustworthy
De is trustworthiness
The sage's heart is open
Breathing in all creation
Connecting with the hearts of all
Drawing together all under heaven
In the perfect oneness of the heart
Restoring all to the innocence of children

Chapter 49 Reflections

The heart is at the center of this chapter, just as it is the center of our being. The character for heart 心 appears five times in this chapter, giving it special emphasis. In Chinese, this character has a broader meaning than it does in English. In English language and thought, the heart and mind are separate, with the heart governing emotion and the mind governing rational thought. But in Chinese, the heart and mind are inextricably joined, because to the Chinese, the heart is the seat not only of emotion but also of discernment and inner wisdom. The character for De 德 has a heart component on the lower right side, so the concept of virtue as used in the *Dao De Jing* is directly connected to the heart.

This heart centeredness is described in the opening passage about being good and trustworthy to all, reflecting the impartial generosity of nature. Flowers reveal their beauty to any and all who pass by, and even when no one is passing by. If nature does not discriminate, then who are we to do so? Whether we act with kindness, compassion, and integrity does not depend on others. In a world that has become so entrenched in dualistic, judgmental polarity, this presents a radically different perspective.

This is the perspective of the sage, whose heart is open to all, without judgment or discrimination. With an open heart, the sage is connected to all in an ocean-like oneness of existence, receiving with gratitude whatever life brings, and offering love to all without exception. In this way, the sage becomes a conduit for the powerful energy of the universe to bestow its loving grace on all beings. This energy is available to all of us at all times. We need not seek it, develop it, or be worthy of it. We need only to release whatever blocks it in our lives. In so doing, we return to the innocence that birthed us into being.

I tell you the truth, unless you change and become like little children, you will never enter the kingdom of heaven.

~Matthew 18:3

Chapter 50

Life emerges into form and returns to formlessness
Three in ten are life's apprentice
Three in ten are death's apprentice
Three in ten live to excess, hastening toward death
We hear of those who hold life's power well
They go forth without fear of wild buffalo or tiger
Enter battle without armor or weapons
Wild buffalo find nowhere to thrust their horns
Tigers find nowhere to sink their claws
Weapons find nowhere their blades can pierce
Why is this
Because there is no place for death

Chapter 50 Reflections

This chapter about living in balanced alignment contains one of my favorite passages in the *Dao De Jing*. I love the vivid imagery of tigers and wild buffalo finding no place to harm a person who lives in powerful harmony with the universe. Although the math is a bit fuzzy, the text suggests that those who live this way are rare. Considering that aligned harmony is our natural state, available to everyone always, why would such alignment be uncommon?

Perhaps we can gain some understanding from two of the characters used in the line about those who hold life's power well.

The first character 闻 means to hear. The inside part 耳 means ear, and the outside part 门 means gate or doorway, so there is a sense of hearing into or through, or perhaps hearing as the gate or doorway to understanding.

The second character 攝 has several meanings including to draw in, gather one's power, maintain prime condition, guard or protect. It breaks down into the left side 扌 meaning hand, and the right side 聶 meaning whisper. The right side comprises three ears, so there is a sense of listening carefully with your full attention, as to a whisper, and protecting or holding on to what you hear.

From these two characters, it's clear that living in aligned harmony with life's power has a lot to do with listening! Not listening to podcasts or gurus or experts but listening within to the wisdom of the universe that whispers in your soul, that whispers in everyone's soul. That, I think, is what accounts for the rarity of people living in alignment. It's not that they are chosen, or special, or better than anyone. It's that they are quiet inside and give their full attention to listening, while most folks are too busy chattering away in their thinking minds. But truth is not a thought, and no amount of thinking will reveal truth. Truth is universal revelation, emerging from the silence through the gateway of a listening spirit into the vast space of an open heart.

In every moment, the Universe is whispering to you. You're constantly surrounded by signs, coincidences, and synchronicities, all aimed at propelling you in the direction of your destiny.

~Denise Linn

Chapter 51

Dao gives birth to all things
De nurtures them
Matter forms them
Conditions complete them
Thus the ten thousand things revere Dao and honor De
Not because it is demanded of them
But because it is natural for them to do so
Just as it is natural for Dao to give birth
And for De to nurture, nourish, and protect
Creating without possessing
Accomplishing without claiming credit
Supporting without dominating
This is the mysterious secret of De

Chapter 51 Reflections

Dao and De dance the story of creation throughout this chapter, Dao as the source of all things and De as the life force that sustains all things. Dao manifests as the universe through the creative agency of De. What is undifferentiated and unlimited potential in the infinite emptiness of Dao springs forth and individuates into the ten thousand things, like a light shining through a prism to create rainbows of different colors.

The relationship between the creative energy of Dao and De, and the created universe of the ten thousand things, is one of tender care and grateful respect. This dynamic is not born of contrived duty and obligation, but rather is the natural dynamic of intrinsic mutuality. It is the nature of Dao to express its inherent beauty and loving perfection through De's transforming energy. And it is the nature of creation to revere and honor the source from which it comes and to which it will return. It requires no effort. It is simply reality.

This natural reality is expressed by the concept of *ziran* meaning self so, or self as it is, or what is naturally so. This concept is foundational in Daoist thought, leading us again and again back to our true nature, which shines effortlessly and radiantly when we remove whatever blocks it. With blocks removed, the inherent power of the universe, with which we are naturally aligned, flows unimpeded through our being. We receive and pass on this nurturing, nourishing, and protective energy. We lead fearless lives of powerful integrity.

We don't need to achieve this natural state. It is simply who we are. But we do need to become aware of and remove whatever blocks its full expression. How do we do this? I sometimes use this acronym to help me remember: WOW

Watch – Stay alert to what arises in the present moment without expectation or trying to control.

Open – Empty your thoughts of judgment and narratives about what arises. Be curious and receptive.

Wait – Respond rather than react. Your heart will know the way forward. Listen for its guidance, trust what you hear, and have the courage to follow it.

WOW also evokes in me an attitude of reverence, awe, and gratitude, the natural response of creation to the gift and miracle of existence.

Oh wow. Oh wow. Oh wow.
~Steve Jobs last words before he died

Chapter 52

All under heaven has a source
This being the mother of all things
To know the mother is to know the child
To know the child is to return to the mother's embrace
Becoming one with the eternal source
And therefore beyond all danger

Close the mouth
Latch the door
Life is untroubled
Open the mouth
Meddle in affairs
Life is lost

Seeing the small is insight
Abiding in tenderness is strength
Using the light within
Restore enlightenment
Protect the self from harm
This is our eternal practice

Chapter 52 Reflections

The image of the divine mother figures prominently in this chapter, giving us the sense that Dao gives birth to, rather than manufactures, all under heaven. The bond between Dao and the universe is intimate and loving, like the bond between mother and child. We connect to the divine source through relationship. This relationship reflects our oneness with all creation.

As with the bond between mother and child, there is an order and reliability in the natural world that we can trust. We sometimes tend to jump in and direct things instead of aligning ourselves with the effortless, perfect, perpetual unfolding of the universe, which takes care of itself and of us when we surrender our own agendas. When we interfere, no matter how well-intentioned, we disrupt this natural flow. Imbalance results, often with unforeseen or unwanted consequences. Then we are caught up in an endless struggle to repair, fix, restore, and basically try to undo what we have done.

When faced with the consequences of our interference, we often wish we could go back to that moment when we first set ourselves on a path out of sync with nature's inherent wisdom. We can't go back, but the universe is generous in giving us many opportunities to choose whether to trust or interfere. Indeed, as the chapter tells us, this is our eternal practice. The character for practice 習 occurs only this one time in the *Dao De Jing*. The top of the character means feathers or wings, and the bottom means pure, white, or bright, suggesting that our practice lifts us up into the pure light of awakening.

Every moment offers us an opportunity to practice. Seeing perfection in the small is a moment of enlightenment. Abiding in tenderness strengthens our heart energy of compassion. We don't practice only when we are on our meditation cushion, or in church, or in martial arts class. Our practice becomes integrated into our daily lives. We practice with every breath, with every heartbeat. Our practice isn't something we do. It becomes who we are, living in harmony with all under heaven, ever embraced in love.

There is no such thing as enlightenment. There are only enlightened moments.

~Adyashanti

Chapter 53

If I have even a little knowledge
I will follow the great path of Dao
Straying from it is my only fear
Dao's path is smooth and easy
Yet people often veer off to the side
While the palace courts are splendid
The fields lie fallow
And the granaries are empty
People wear elegant clothes
And carry sharp weapons
Eating and drinking to excess
Hoarding their wealth and possessions
This extravagance is like stealing
It is not the great path of Dao

Chapter 53 Reflections

This chapter is one that many of us can relate to. We know what is important, but we are so easily distracted. Whether it's entertainment, worries, obligations, social media, or one more email, deadline, text, episode of our favorite show, or piece of pie, we allow ourselves to get caught up in the shiny object of the moment and lose our centered alignment with the great path of Dao.

What is so alluring about all these sideroads? Perhaps we are carried along by trends, or seek some immediate gratification, or need some relief from burdens. I suspect that many of our digressions are compelled by some underlying fear of the unknown. The path of Dao is not one of certainty; it is a path walked in trust, listening to our inner guidance.

How then do we bring ourselves back into alignment when we have strayed? The character in the second line translated as "follow" 行 can also mean to walk, travel, or move forward. The left side means to take a step forward, and the right side means small steps.

This suggests that we walk the great path of Dao one small step at a time. Trying to see what is further down the road can lead to anxiety. Maybe we can't see around a bend, or perhaps the road just seems too long. We lose our focus and our resolve, we get caught up in our thoughts, and we are easily drawn off course. It happens. But when we sink our energy out of our chattering mind down into our quiet center, when we bring our attention back to the ground under our feet, we realize that we know everything we need to take the next step. And the next one.

Yes, this is sometimes a challenge. We look around and see the descriptions of society written 2,500 years ago reflected in our world today. This chapter has timeless relevance to the human condition. We can feel overwhelmed or discouraged, and perhaps sometimes a little envious of those who seem to be living high. That too is a sideroad off the great path. What can we do? Take the next small step on the path. And the next one. It always comes back to that. With time, the path begins to glow more beautifully than all the shiny distractions along the way, and we find that indeed, it is smooth and easy.

> *Whether you turn to the right or to the left, your ears will hear a voice behind you, saying, "This is the way; walk in it."*
>
> ~Isaiah 30:21

Chapter 54

What is well planted cannot be uprooted
What is embraced in the heart cannot be stripped away
Generations honor this legacy
When we cultivate this perfection
In the self, De becomes genuine
In the family, De becomes overflowing
In the community, De becomes everlasting
In the nation, De becomes abundant
In the universe, De becomes omnipresent
Thus the self reveals the self
The family reveals the family
The community reveals the community
The nation reveals the nation
The universe reveals the universe
By this all things are known

Chapter 54 Reflections

This chapter beautifully expresses the nature of De in every aspect of the universe. It is the perfect form of the formless, the perfect creation emerging from the origin of creation. It is the natural alignment within all realms, all parts connected, all parts resonating in harmony.

The *Dao De Jing* describes an approach to life that is contrary to the way many of us operate. We often move from the outside to the inside. We manufacture an external structure of rules to govern ourselves, from the nation to the individual, and then we are obligated to follow the rules, subject to enforcement by others. This internal obedience to external regulation, so the theory goes, leads to peace and harmony at all levels of existence. However, it doesn't take much to see that this system generates the need for more and more rules as circumstances change and new situations arise, as well as ever increasing enforcement measures.

When we begin inside the individual, however, and move outward, we get a very different model. When I am internally aligned with the unhindered flow of Dao, then De naturally and effortlessly manifests through me. As this internal resonance vibrates outwardly, the family, community, nation, and universe, all become aligned in harmony, reflecting the natural order of all creation.

That might sound idealistic and overwhelming, considering the discord and polarization we witness all around us, but I've found it has practical application. When my kids were growing up, there were inevitable periods of disharmony. After futile attempts to impose order, I discovered that if I started by centering myself, bringing myself into peaceful alignment, the level of agitation in the family would start to drop. It was like everyone remembered how to breathe. And then the way forward would become evident.

How do we cultivate this perfection within ourselves? De is the manifestation of our natural resonance with the universe. We don't need to practice it. What we practice is releasing everything that blocks it. We don't need to change who we are; we simply need to *be* who we are. We do this by seeing everything as it is, seeing ourselves as we are, and knowing that all is well.

All shall be well, and all shall be well, and all manner of thing shall be well.

~Julian of Norwich

Chapter 55

The full embodiment of Dao
Is like a newborn babe
Poisonous insects do not sting
Fierce beasts do not attack
Predator birds do not strike
Its bones are yielding and its muscles tender
Yet its grasp is unbreakable
It knows not the union of male and female
Yet its wholeness is complete
Its life force is at its zenith
It wails all day without getting hoarse
It abides in perfect harmony
Knowing harmony is eternal
Knowing eternal is enlightenment
Life's expansion of energy is auspicious
The heart's liberation of qi is powerful
Forms manifest and return in natural cycles
Interference disrupts harmony
This is not Dao's way

Chapter 55 Reflections

The chapter begins with a passage comparing a person with abundant De to an infant, a metaphor repeated several times in the *Dao De Jing*. A baby is supple and soft, yet amazingly strong and full of vigor. A baby's innocent and unfiltered engagement with life in the present moment is its protection, its power, and its wisdom. It lives in perfect harmony. This is reflected in Jesus's encouragement to be like a small child, to whom the kingdom of heaven belongs. And it is echoed in *A Course in Miracles*, which teaches that our safety lies in our defenselessness.

The inherent power of this life force that energizes and expands all creation is suggested by three characters in this chapter, all using a root component that means rice 米 or rice stalk 禾: 精 life force, 和 harmony, and 氣 qi. Rice is a symbol of fertility and abundance, so its use in characters has a very favorable connotation. In the character for qi, rice is combined with a component meaning air. The image is one of rice cooking, creating steam, a powerful image to represent our vital and nourishing life force.

This chapter has a surprise bonus, a little hidden wisdom treasure.

Life's expansion of energy is auspicious
The heart's liberation of qi is powerful

These two lines can also be translated in a contrasting way:

Increasing life energy can be ominous
The mind's control of qi can overstrain

Which is right? Several characters in these lines are susceptible to different meanings and support either view, revealing the beauty and unfathomable paradox of Dao.

Despite appearances, the two translations are not in conflict with each other. When we are aligned with Dao, our energy is uncontained and unrestricted. It moves in concert with the energy of the universe. Our power is unlimited because it is not our individual power, but universal power, moving through us as it manifests and expands. When we seek to impose our individual will on this energy, however, especially in our attempts to deny the natural cycles of creation, the effort we expend depletes our vital energy and leads to disharmony and misfortune. While formlessness is eternal, form manifests and returns. We are both finite and infinite.

Babies are not troubled by this. No wonder so many wisdom teachings honor them.

And a little child shall lead them.

~Isaiah 11:6

Chapter 56

One who knows does not speak
One who speaks does not know
Seal the openings
Close the door
Blunt the point
Unravel the knots
Soften the brightness
Become one with the dust
This is called mysterious union
This union is beyond attachment and aversion
Beyond gain and loss
Beyond honor and disgrace
It embraces all creation

Chapter 56 Reflections

After reading the opening lines, our first instinct might be to be quiet, to show, or at least hope, that we are among those who know. But then, after a while, we want to talk about it, either to share what we think we know, or to question whether we know anything at all. Even Lao Zi, the purported author of the *Dao De Jing*, acknowledges in the first chapter that the Dao defies identification and understanding...and then proceeds to use roughly 5,000 characters to describe it.

Our minds operate in the realm of thought, and we communicate using language. Yet these two functions, by their very nature, take us a step away from the direct and unfiltered experience of reality. That doesn't mean that thinking and speaking are bad. Our brains are wired to identify, label, evaluate, categorize, and file away. That's just what brains do. It does mean, though, that our thoughts, silent or spoken, will inevitably fail, like Moses, to accompany us into the promised land of awakened experience. Our aim in thinking and speaking might be, then, as Adyashanti says, to fail well.

The chapter invites us to explore our relationship with thought and speech by slowing things down, pausing, softening our quest for certainty, and allowing our natural unity with the source of all creation to reveal itself. Entering the "promised land" is not achieved by effort or force. In fact, it is not achieved at all because in truth we never left it. We wake up and remember that we are exactly where we've always been – safe at home in the embrace of all creation.

The mystery of oneness is experienced with our whole being rather than discovered through intellectual thought. But of course, once experienced, we want to talk about it! We are human, after all. There is no need to take a vow of silence, but we can pause occasionally and open space for the mystery to peek in and say hello.

Knowledge speaks but wisdom listens.
~often attributed to Jimi Hendrix

Chapter 57

One can rule a country with strict rules
One can wage war with surprise strategy
But one can master the power of the universe only with
    noninterference
How do I know this is so
By this
With more regulation people are more impoverished
With more sharp weapons the nation is more troubled
With more laws more criminals appear
Therefore the sage says
I refrain from forcing change
And people transform themselves
I abide in stillness
And people guide themselves
I refrain from interfering
And people flourish by themselves
I live without desire
And people content themselves

Chapter 57 Reflections

The theme of this chapter is simple: Do not interfere.

We don't have to look far to see where interference, even well-intentioned, has caused more harm than good. In the southern United States, you can see miles and miles of natural vegetation suffocated by the uncontrollable proliferation of kudzu, a non-indigenous plant introduced along roadways to prevent erosion. These efforts to prevent erosion have now resulted in even more strenuous and costly efforts to contain the devastation caused by the kudzu.

When we encounter unanticipated results of interfering, we often feel an urge to "fix" things by interfering even more. I can see how some of my own efforts to help and then to fix resulting problems have created only more issues to resolve.

Apparently, this fix it, fix it more, fix it better, mentality is not new. This chapter, written over 2,000 years ago, acknowledges the futility of all our attempts to control others, to control circumstances, to control ourselves. Where does this urge to interfere come from? It must start with some judgment about what is good and what is bad. What makes me think I know enough to make that distinction? Does making the distinction in itself create the need to fix whatever I have judged as bad?

If I look beneath that judgment, I will most likely find fear. In a curious quirk of the English language, "do not interfere," if said aloud, sounds just like "do not enter fear." What happens if I breathe into the fear with compassion and trust the natural unfolding of the universe? The last part of the chapter describes this natural unfolding with repeated use of the character for self, suggesting that there is a natural self-management throughout all of creation if we can find the courage to trust it and let it be. What a relief to be freed from the responsibility of being chief operating officer of our own lives and the lives of others, a responsibility that has never been ours and that we can never fulfill.

Yesterday I was clever so I wanted to change the world. Today I am wise so I am changing myself.

~Rumi

I might amend that last sentence: Today I am wise so I will trust myself and all of creation with loving acceptance.

Chapter 58

When government is unobtrusive
People are wholesome and sincere
When government is oppressive
People are restless and contentious
Good fortune arises in the ashes of calamity
Misery is held in the folds of joy's robes
Who knows their limits
Without balanced alignment
Government becomes perverted
Benevolence becomes distorted
People lose their way
Their confusion becomes entrenched
Thus the sage stays aligned and does not divide
Incorruptible yet without judgment
Consistent yet not severe
Illuminating yet not blinding

Chapter 58 Reflections

This chapter highlights the folly of thinking that we know what is good or bad, or that we can control things outside of ourselves.

The *Dao De Jing's* passages on government align with the view that the "government is best that governs least," or with the concept of the "servant leader." This is challenging to apply in today's world where the more traditional social structures of villages and small communities are missing in much of the developed world. I prefer to consider these government passages in relation to our own individual self-government. Then the message of the text is easier to discern and apply.

When I am overly harsh with self-criticism or overly strict with rigid rules, especially rules that are externally generated, I lose my connection with the natural energy that moves all around me and within me. If instead, I remain fluid and in alignment with this energy, then, to borrow from Buddhist terminology, "right action" spontaneously and effortlessly manifests through me.

The Chinese characters illustrate this beautifully. The character 淳, used in relation to an unobtrusive government, means wholesome and sincere. The three little lines on the left side of the character, meaning water, form the radical or root of this word, conveying a sense of fluid purity. In contrast, the character 缺, used in relation to an oppressive government, means restless or contentious. The left side of the character means jar and the right side means broken, conveying a sense of brittleness or fragments.

An oppressive government, when referring to the self, suggests an attitude of unbending self-judgment, which often expresses as judgment of others as well. It assumes a certainty about what is right and wrong, or good and bad. But when we look at the characters for misery 祸 and good fortune 福, we see on the left the same radical 礻 meaning to show or reveal, as in a sacred revelation, suggesting that good fortune and misery are both rooted in holy origin, both part of the divine dance of life.

Our grasping at one and avoidance of the other deny their interconnectedness and leave us off balance and confused. On the other hand, when we drop our judgments of good and bad, and our attachment to pleasure and aversion to pain, we can see everything as it is, we can accept things as they are, we can accept ourselves as we are. We can regain the natural fluidity of our internal balanced alignment, integrated, whole, pure, and enlightened.

Outer world is just the mirror image of your inner world.

~Amit Ray

Chapter 59

For governing in alignment with heaven
Nothing compares with moderation
Moderation from the beginning
Leads to abundant accumulation of De
Abundant accumulation of De
Leads to mastery without limits
With limitless mastery
One can govern with a mother's enduring care
Such enduring care sinks deep roots
Of Dao's eternal vision

Chapter 59 Reflections

"Everything in moderation," as the saying goes. The Noble Eightfold Path of Buddhism is described as "the middle way." A common instruction in both meditation and taiji is "not too tight, not too loose." Moderation is a theme in wisdom traditions and is the theme of this chapter. It begins by advocating moderation in governing people. As with other chapters on governing, I find the concept most helpful in the context of self-governance. How does moderation guide us in our own lives?

The character for moderation 嗇 has components that mean earth, people, from, return, upright, and entrance. That is a lot to pack into one character! Returning, we are told elsewhere in the *Dao De Jing*, is the motion of Dao. There is a natural cycle of manifesting into form and returning to formlessness, or coming from the dust of the earth and returning to the earth, or the simple cycle of breathing as we inhale and exhale. Moderation is the alignment with this natural cycle, the balancing and connecting energy of the two movements.

The practice of moderation is not forced. Our aligned self-governance is not judgmental but rather rooted in deep self-acceptance and self-love. It is as natural as a mother's care. Three characters in this line about the deep roots of enduring care have tree components 木, suggesting the strength and dignity of a great tree. The tree does not strive or toil. It aligns with its environment and lives in harmony.

We can experience the connection between the middle way of moderation and the sacred energy moving between heaven and earth like the tree that has its roots in the earth and its apical meristem in the heavens. When we swing too far in one direction, we lose this alignment and must then use energy to maintain the imbalance. Or we swing too far to the other extreme to compensate. Either way, we are expending a lot of energy to hold an unsustainable position.

The middle way of moderation, however, attunes us to our inner guidance as it cascades like a waterfall through the chapter and through our lives, accumulating abundant De, leading effortlessly to mastery without limits.

Moderation is the silken string running through the pearl chain of all virtues.

~Joseph Hall

Chapter 60

Govern a big country like frying small fish
Follow Dao to rule everything under heaven
Then demons are rendered powerless
Dao has great power
Yet its power does no harm
The sage's power also does no harm
Together they do no harm
Thus De is integrated and restored

Chapter 60 Reflections

Not being much of a cook myself, I consulted friends about how to cook small fish so that I could better understand this analogy. The consensus was basically that less is more. That is, cook for a short time with minimum stirring or turning. Too much fussing will overcook or break the fish. This is consistent with other passages in the *Dao De Jing* about governing, and applies just as well to governing ourselves.

Recently, I was struggling with a situation that churned up a lot of emotion for me. My initial response was to try to control things, to direct the outcome of my choice by convincing others that I was right, or at least forcing them to comply with my wishes. Not surprisingly, I was not very successful, and even to the extent that I was, my emotional turmoil was not alleviated.

Finally, I just stopped fighting. I let go of what I couldn't control, which of course was everything outside myself, and focused instead on regaining my internal alignment and equanimity. As soon as I released my self-righteous and aggressive interference, everything began to unfold in a natural way. True, not everything was entirely to my liking, but I could appreciate that much of what happened was inevitable and perhaps even for the best. Peace was restored.

Furthermore, I realized that my earlier agitation had less to do with the circumstances themselves, and a lot more to do with my desire for relief from my own anxiety and fear. I saw that my anxiety and fear resulted from the narrative I was telling myself about what was happening and the anticipated calamitous outcome, neither of which was based in reality. Basically, I created my own demons. When I realigned myself with Dao, the demons had no power.

I'm learning to cook small fish for dinner.

Good food is often, even most often, simple food.
~Anthony Bourdain

Chapter 61

A great nation is like a river delta
All streams converge at the lowest point
Manifesting the receptive stillness of yin energy
Absorbing the power of all the water that flows into it
Thus a great nation places itself below a small nation
Thereby drawing to it the small nation
As the small nation joins the power of the great nation
The great nation cares for its people
As the small nation is protected
Each obtains the highest benefit by mutual humility

Chapter 61 Reflections

This chapter addresses the theme of power in the context of the relationship between large and small countries. It applies just as well to relationships between people and invites us to explore how we govern ourselves and how we interact with others.

The *Dao De Jing* often uses the image of water to describe the natural movement and energy of Dao. Water naturally flows toward the lowest point. As a river flows toward the sea, it gathers the energy from all the tributaries that flow into it, so that when it reaches its lowest point, it is at its most powerful, and becomes more powerful still as it merges with the vastness of the ocean.

The harmonious relationship between large and small countries is fostered not by force but by mutual respect and humility. The character for low 下 is used nine times in this chapter and can also mean underneath or humble. This reminds me of the custom in some cultures of greeting others by bowing, each party offering humble respect rather than demanding it. Bowing is often a part of martial arts ritual. Teachers and students bow to each other. Higher and lower ranked students bow to each other. Sparring partners bow to each other before and after combat. I have always appreciated this aspect of my training, instilling in me a respect for others as well as for the training itself.

Humility is sometimes perceived as weakness or passivity or being taken advantage of. But that is a confusion with humiliation. Humiliation is an injury to ego, whereas humility is a relinquishment of ego. Humility has a quality of strength and power, like the power of the ocean that lies below all the waters of the earth.

True power comes not from force, but from alignment with the natural energy of the universe, allowing that energy to flow unimpeded. I once watched a small, elderly, taiji master easily dispatch attacks from younger, bigger, stronger, highly skilled martial artists. He was demonstrating the humble power of the ocean.

Humility is a quality we used to value. It is one of the fruits of the spirit listed in the Bible. But as we look around today, it seems that self-promotion and self-aggrandizement are the coin of the realm. This chapter invites us to contemplate the value of humility in our own lives when we check our ego at the door and bow to the beauty of every moment's blessing.

Blessed are the meek, for they shall inherit the earth.
~Matthew 5:5

Chapter 62

Dao is the honored source of all creation
The awakened person treasures it
The unenlightened are protected by it
Greater than emperors and ministers
More valuable than precious jade
Is sitting quietly and offering Dao to the world
From ancient times Dao has been revered
For those who seek receive
And are released from their mistakes
Thus is Dao treasured by all under heaven

Chapter 62 Reflections

This chapter is an ode to the natural beauty and humble majesty of Dao, treasured by those who recognize it and tenderly protecting those who don't. There is no judgment in that distinction. As the joke goes, "What's the difference between an enlightened person and an unenlightened person? The unenlightened person thinks there's a difference." All are equal before the loving generosity of the universe.

Wisdom teachings from all traditions offer a "better way" or a "different way." All aspire to liberate us from the suffering we cause ourselves by our unenlightened thoughts, words, and actions. And all offer assurance that relief is ours for the asking. So what keeps us from asking? When I consider the choice between on one hand holding on to the "precious jade" of my opinions, judgments, fears, resentments, anger, and unforgiveness, and on the other hand accepting the boundless riches of my natural inheritance, it doesn't seem like a tough choice. But still....

When contemplating this chapter, I became aware of a resentment I was holding against someone. I knew that it was blocking my own joy and separating me from divine union, but still there was something about it I savored. I liked to talk about it with others, to get sympathy and to reinforce my righteous outrage. I would start to let it go and then snatch it back again, not quite done with feeling betrayed and hurt.

And then, sitting on my meditation cushion trying all the techniques I know to ease my grip on what I knew was causing my own suffering, I suddenly saw an image. In this image I was underwater, sinking with the weight of a rock I was grasping. I treasured this rock and did not want to let it go. But as I sank further from the surface, the value of the rock began to fade as my desire for the light and air above became more urgent. Finally, as you can guess, I wanted to rise back to the surface and breathe that precious air more than I wanted anything else. The rock was killing me, and as much as I had valued it, I now cared nothing for it and let it go.

If we really understood what our choice is, we would drop like a hot potato anything that blocks our true and only real treasure. We would, as Pema Chödrön says, practice like our hair is on fire. We would live in humble gratitude and deep joy.

For where your treasure is, there will your heart be also.

~Matthew 6:21

Chapter 63

Act without acting
Engage without engaging
Know without knowing
Whether big small many few
Respond to all injury with De
Prepare for the difficult while still easy
Undertake the big while still small
All difficult matters have easy beginnings
All big accomplishments begin with small steps
Thus the sage stays humble
Thereby achieving great things
Avoiding the arrogance of false promises
The sage effortlessly completes what is needed

Chapter 63 Reflections

The opening lines of this chapter express the paradox of Dao, especially the first line which returns to the theme of *wu wei*, or non-action. How do we act without acting? When we are fully present and respond naturally to our circumstances rather than trying to force other people or events to conform to how we think things should be, we have a sense that action is happening through us but not by us. This ability to respond naturally results from an inner alignment and harmony with reality, which allows us to be fully present and to respond appropriately rather than to force or react.

From this place of alignment, we naturally respond to any injury with De. This is a concept that transcends kindness or forgiveness, but rather describes the perspective and manifestation of a unified view of all creation, without judgment or fear. This relationship is represented so beautifully by the characters for injury and De.

The character for injury 怨 breaks down into a top half that means to turn over, as when you are asleep, and a bottom half that means heart. You could say that all injury, big or small, many or few, results from a heart that has "turned over" as if asleep. In contrast, the character for De 德 includes the same heart component we find in the first character combined with other components meaning to go forward and aligned vision. This conveys a sense of going forward guided by the inner vision of the heart. This guidance leads us in appropriate response regardless of the nature of the injury.

A Course in Miracles teaches that everything we do or think or say is without exception one of two things: a call for love or an expression of love. When we misperceive ourselves as separate and in conflict, we often call for love through anger, judgment, fear, manipulation. It is like our heart has turned over and gone to sleep. Conversely, when our heart is awake, we correctly perceive ourselves as universally connected and in harmony. We are guided by the inner vision of the heart, and love is expressed through us and out into the world. Love is transformed into the gift of grace effortlessly, perfectly, beautifully. This is the essence of acting without acting.

> *Hatred never ceases by hatred but by love alone is healed.*
> ~the Buddha

Chapter 64

Peace is easily sustained
Not yet begun is easily planned
Brittle is easily broken
Finely ground is easily scattered
Act from emptiness
Manage before trouble arises

A tree too wide to embrace grows from a tiny seed
A tower of nine levels rises from a mound of dirt
A journey of a thousand miles begins under the foot

Force leads to failure
Grasping leads to loss
Thus the sage forces not and does not fail
Grasps not and does not lose

People falter as completion nears
So take care at the end as at the beginning

Thus the sage desires no desire
Studies no learning
Does not treasure material things
Allows the ten thousand things to be as they are
Never presumes to interfere

Chapter 64 Reflections

This chapter seems to contain several independent sections, each one conveying its own message. And one can certainly read it that way, contemplating the wisdom of each section separately.

My favorite line in this chapter, for example, is the familiar saying about a long journey. It is often translated as "A journey of a thousand miles begins with a single step." Rather than a "single step," however, the characters literally mean "under the foot." This gives the proverb a slightly different meaning. No matter where I'm headed, my location is always exactly under my feet. No matter how many steps I take, whether walking across the room or on a journey of a thousand miles, I am always in the same place, that is, over my feet. The present moment, standing on this ground, is where I exist.

If there is a theme in this chapter, however, it might be that everything big starts small. A journey is taken one step at a time. Trouble can best be avoided before it takes hold. A great project is planned before work begins and accomplished in manageable stages. Things have a way of naturally unfolding and evolving when we stay centered and focused. Like a great tree growing from a tiny seed, our actions then arise from this alignment, empty of ego. We no longer create suffering with ego-driven forcing or grasping. We allow things to be as they are, without trying to control or interfere.

In this way, peace is indeed easily sustained. That might seem unrealistic considering how elusive peace has been throughout history and up to the present time. Peace often seems just as elusive in our personal lives. Whether individual or collective, conflict is always caused when there is a shift out of alignment due to fear, which might manifest as anger, judgment, aggression, or righteousness. This fear arises from our mistaken belief in separation from each other and from the natural order and harmony of the universe. It then extends outward into our lives. But when we remember who we are, we are "re-membered," awakened to our interconnectedness with the ten thousand things and with the source of all creation. Conflict dissipates and inner peace is restored.

When feelings, tasks, or circumstances threaten to overwhelm us, we are encouraged by this chapter to focus on the small, the present moment, the ground under our feet. We can breathe into our distress, relax our bodies, release our urge to control or interfere, take the one seat in the center of our lives, and trust that all will unfold according to the natural order of the universe.

*Never be in a hurry; do everything quietly and in a calm spirit.
Do not lose your inner peace for anything whatsoever,
even if your whole world seems upset.*

~Saint Francis de Sales

Chapter 65

In ancient times rulers who followed Dao
Did not teach people to be clever
But rather encouraged people to follow their true nature
Governing by manipulation brought ruin
But governing in alignment with Dao brought good fortune
To know the difference between these two
Is called profound De
Profound De extends deep and far
Linking all things to the source
Thus attaining perfect harmony

Chapter 65 Reflections

I have taken great liberty with the translation here because the use of certain characters in this chapter seems atypical in the context of the *Dao De Jing*. So with apologies to those who prefer a more literal approach, I hope I have captured the essential message of the chapter, which expresses a theme threading through the entire text. That is, nature has its own wisdom that we cannot improve on, and when we try, our interference causes chaos and suffering.

When I was raising my kids, I'm sure I more closely resembled the ruler who governed, if not by manipulation, certainly by expectation and enforced rules. I was more concerned about shaping nature rather than allowing true nature to unfold. My approach might not have brought ruin, thank goodness, but it was exhausting.

Maybe I'm just getting too tired as I get older to expend a lot of energy trying to force things to be a certain way. I find that when I allow things to run their natural course, everything turns out all right. In hindsight, I see the wisdom inherent in the unhindered unfolding of the universe, even if at an earlier stage it seemed that everything was going the wrong way. "Wrong," of course, according to me and my limited vision and anxiety at the time.

I'm learning to suspend judgment and take the approach voiced by a friend: "Let's just see what happens." When I'm able to do that, all the moving pieces do indeed seem to settle into harmonious resonance. I've come to appreciate the perfection of outcomes that I neither planned nor anticipated.

Trust the process.

~Kyle Cline

Chapter 66

The sea is king of a hundred valleys
Because its goodness lies below them it can rule over them
One who would rule others must support them from underneath
One who would lead others must encourage them from behind
Thus the sage dwells above yet people are not burdened
Stays ahead yet people are not hindered
All under heaven delight in endless joy
Because the sage neither strives nor struggles
No one can contend against him

Chapter 66 Reflections

This beautiful chapter is about leadership, comparing a good leader to the sea, abiding patiently in the lowest position, allowing all water to return home according to its own path. The opening passage blends two thematic images for Dao – water and valleys. The valley is open, receptive, guiding the water that flows through it and nourishing all that grows in its embrace. Water's energy comes from following its nature, flowing in harmony with gravity, around and over or under all obstacles, returning to its source in the vast ocean. In both cases, the valley's power of nurturing and the ocean's power of ruling come from assuming a humble position.

This reminds me of the Bible passage that says those who are first shall be last, and those who are last shall be first, thus describing the concept of the servant leader. When a leader understands this principle, the chapter goes on to observe that the people are neither burdened nor hindered. Good leadership embodies humility, not arrogance.

When we contend or strive, we divide ourselves into winners and losers. In so doing, we lose the opportunity for connection, for relationship, for peace. The character for contend 争 breaks down into the top that means horn, the middle that means snout, and the vertical line with the hook at the bottom. It reminds me of a bull being led by a ring in its nose. Visually, the character looks unstable, standing precariously on that point at the bottom, struggling or striving to maintain its balance. When we strive or struggle, we are like that bull, hooked by something that pulls us off balance so that we are easily controlled.

When we do not contend, however, we are like water that does not strive, yet eludes attempts to push it, grab it, or force it. It achieves its purpose effortlessly, in harmony with all nature. When we live according to our true nature, in harmony and humility, we open a channel for the energy of the universe to flow into us and manifest through us into the world. We become leaders, repairers of the breach. And nothing is more powerful than that.

You shall raise up the foundations of many generations; you shall be called repairers of the breach, the restorer of streets to dwell in.

~Isaiah 58:12

Chapter 67

All under heaven call my path great
It seems unlike all others
Its greatness rests on this singularity
If it resembled others it would indeed be insignificant
I have three treasures which I guard and cherish
First is compassion
Second is simplicity
Third is humility
Compassion generates courage
Simplicity allows generosity
Humility creates enduring potential
When compassion is renounced
    Yet courage is contrived
When simplicity is abandoned
    Yet generosity is pretended
When humility is forsaken
    Yet enduring potential is claimed
Death follows
Compassion brings victory in conflict
And strength in protection
What heaven creates
Compassion enfolds

Chapter 67 Reflections

This chapter invites us to explore our own "treasures," because, as the Bible tells us, "For where your treasure is, there your heart will be also." Adyashanti describes these treasures as "soul values," which form a bridge between the experience of the infinite ground of undifferentiated beingness and the experience of being embodied in an incarnated form. In other words, how do we live transcendent awakening in our daily lives?

Soul values include those mentioned in this chapter. Identifying your treasure isn't about discovering a magic secret, but rather about discerning what is most essential to you. What values resonate in your soul, guide your choices, carry you through difficult times, and open your heart to all the blessings of this life? They don't have to always be the same. As your life unfolds, they might evolve as well.

For me, I identified trust, surrender, and union. When we identify and align with our soul values, their benefits naturally manifest. For example, in my life, trust generates fearlessness, surrender leads to liberation, and union expands to embrace all creation with love.

The chapter cautious us, however, that the qualities generated by our treasures don't always work in reverse. An easy example might be that false modesty does not originate in humility but rather in arrogance. The "death" that follows mistaken attempts to adhere to artificial values is not literal, of course. It means that being false in any way drains our life force and empties our soul of its intrinsic strength. Conversely, when we are expressing our true nature, the power of the universe flows through us and out into the world. Effortlessly. Beautifully. Perfectly.

I especially appreciate the emphasis on compassion at the end of the chapter. Like the Bible says about faith, hope, and love, "the greatest of these is love."

My religion is kindness.

~the Dalai Lama

Chapter 68

A good officer is not violent
A good fighter is not angry
A good victory requires no battle
A good leader is humble
Not striving is De's virtue
It is a leader's strength
In alignment with heaven's perfection

Chapter 68 Reflections

This chapter is about power and the use of power. The ancient treatise *The Art of War* counsels that the most successful victory is won without engaging the enemy in battle. This sounds counterintuitive, but I've witnessed the truth of this lesson in my own life.

Because I practice martial arts, folks sometimes ask if I could defend myself against physical attack. Thankfully, the few times that I've perceived a threat of violence, I used my ninja weapons of demeanor, tone, and words to de-escalate the situation and walk away unharmed. My training allowed me to stay calm, centered, alert, unafraid, and ready to respond to whatever was happening.

As a martial art, taiji is closely aligned with the *Dao De Jing*. It's no accident, I think, that the character used for perfection 极 at the end of this chapter is the second character used for the martial art taiji 太极 which means something like the great ultimate. The character breaks down into the left part meaning tree and the right part meaning to extend or reach. To me, this suggests the natural, unstoppable power of a tree expanding through its roots and branches, relying on its own inherent energy rather than external force.

One of Aesop's fables tells of a competition between the wind and the sun to see who was more powerful. Observing a man walking down the road, they agreed that the first one to remove the man's coat would be the victor. The wind blew a fiercely cold gale, but the man just pulled his coat around him more tightly. Finally, the wind was exhausted and stopped. The sun took its turn and simply shone warmly. The man grew hot and removed his coat.

This fable is one of my favorites because it teaches not only that force is not as powerful as gentleness, but also that force exhausts the one expending it. Consider this next time you are trying to get a two-year-old to do anything.

This chapter invites us to explore our own relationship to power. We often equate power with "power over" something or someone. But here we learn that the power of brute force is short-lived and rarely leads to the outcome we desire. We can see in our world that force, while perhaps sometimes unavoidable, never leads to lasting peace. So consider the source of true power and how it manifests in your life.

The day the power of love overrules the love of power, the world will know peace.

~often attributed to Gandhi

Chapter 69

Warriors have a saying
I do not presume to act as host
*   But rather as a guest*
Rather than advance an inch
*   Better to retreat a foot*
Proceed without insisting
Repel without arms
Seize without weapons
Capture without hostility
The greatest mistake is treating conflict lightly
Such carelessness risks losing my treasure
Thus when opposing forces meet
Compassion brings true victory

Chapter 69 Reflections

The subject of power and conflict in the last chapter is continued here. The warrior describes the best strategy as one of nonaggression, preferring instead to respond to rather than initiate attack.

In my early years of practicing martial arts, my tendency in sparring was to go on the offense, immediately and forcefully. I did this because I was afraid. Aggression gave me the illusion of control, and I often persisted even when it was clearly not to my advantage. I've learned over time to take a different approach. My practice now is to empty myself out, remain emotionally detached, and be alert and responsive to what is happening. When I release the urge to force a particular outcome, I am better able to respond naturally and effectively. I can stay centered and do what needs to be done without escalating hostility.

As in martial arts, so in life. As soon as I label someone an enemy, I have separated myself from that person and established an adversarial dynamic that leads to a win/lose battle. We might win a battle, but we have not created a foundation for peace. The most powerful social transformations with lasting impact have been led by courageous people advocating and practicing nonviolence: Martin Luther King, Jr., Gandhi, Nelson Mandela, the Dalai Lama, to name a few. Movements led by violence might achieve temporary dominance, but they inevitably empower resistance and fail the test of time.

In our current culture, we are so locked into an us/them mindset that we cannot see what is lost by the adversarial stance we take with our families, our politics, our legal system, our religion, and our planet. As this chapter so poignantly warns, we lose the treasures we claim to hold dear. Think of the values that are most important to you. Consider whether they are compatible with an aggressive, competitive attitude toward life. My treasures are trust, surrender, and union. These all involve connection, not separation. I've learned that I can have healthy boundaries and still have an open heart, a willing spirit, and faith in the basic goodness of the universe.

This chapter ends with a statement about the supremacy of compassion. There is a saying that the best defense is a good offense. I wonder if instead, the best defense is no offense.

Compassion is revolution.
~bumper sticker

Chapter 70

My words are easy to understand
And very easy to practice
Yet no one under heaven can understand them
No one can put them into practice
Words have origins
Actions have causes
Without understanding this
You cannot know me
Those who know me are few
Those who follow me are rare
Thus the sage hides jade inside ordinary clothes

Chapter 70 Reflections

When I was asked to give a presentation on Daoism to a study group comparing major religions of the world, I was a bit stumped. My first hurdle was to question whether Daoism can rightly be called a religion. As stated in the first chapter of the *Dao De Jing*, the Dao that can be understood or explained is not the eternal Dao. It has no creed, no doctrine, no structure, no ritual, no eligibility requirements. True, there is a Daoist religion that has evolved over time, but it arguably has little relation to the teachings of the *Dao De Jing*, much like some other religions that seem to have gone far afield from their origins.

Bruce Lee described his approach to martial arts as the way of no way. To me, this best captures the essential quality of Dao's wisdom. It is, I explained to the study group, as easy and natural as breathing. In fact, breathing is our best model of Dao in action. Breathe in, breathe out. Manifest into form and return to formlessness. Fluid like water. Easy, just like the chapter says. Why is it so easy? Almost a thousand years ago, Li Hsi-Chai said, "It is easy because there is no Dao to discuss, no knowledge to learn, no effort to make, no deeds to perform."

Then why don't more people understand and follow it? As Li His-Chai continues to explain, "It is hard because the Dao cannot be discussed, because all words are wrong, because it can't be learned, and because the mind only leads us astray." Doesn't that perfectly capture the human brain's frustration when it's not able to name, classify, analyze, evaluate, and attain intellectual clarity and moral conviction? Descartes' famous quote "I think therefore I am" gives us the great mental pleasure of certainty. But the cautionary book title "Don't Believe Everything You Think" throws us right back into the terrifying unknown, terrifying to the brain at least.

So how, then, are we to understand this easy teaching? What does it look like in our lives? Like this: Breathe in, breathe out. Repeat.

For my yoke is easy, and my burden is light.

~Jesus

Chapter 71

Understanding that we do not know is wisdom
Believing that we know the unknowable is suffering
Only when we are sick of suffering
Do we free ourselves from suffering
By understanding the wisdom of not knowing
The sage has awakened from suffering
And is thus liberated

Chapter 71 Reflections

This almost untranslatable chapter proves its own point about suffering. It is concise and cryptic in the extreme. I can tell you from personal experience that efforts to "know" the most accurate translation do indeed lead to suffering. But while a literal translation eludes understanding, the gist of the chapter is clear. Our quest to know, our attachment to belief, our defense of illusion, all lead in one way or another to conscious or unconscious distress.

This is illustrated by the character for suffering 病, which also means sickness of body or spirit, fault, or imperfection. This character is repeated eight times in this short chapter, so it becomes the focal point of contemplation. The top line and the vertical curved line on the left side create a partial enclosure within which is a component meaning inside, showing a person with legs inside a box. To me, this suggests a connection between suffering and the illusion of being stuck or trapped. The right side of the character is wide open, but when we are trapped by our own attachment to knowing, we can't see the open door of liberation from our suffering.

Buddha understood that attachment or desire is the root of suffering. One of the things our brains are wired to seek is unchanging certainty. So strong is the craving that our brains will grasp onto a false answer rather than tolerate the discomfort of not knowing. Once securely attached to an answer, our brains resist the anxiety of releasing it even when a better answer is presented. This leads to suffering, because on some level we know that we are floating in an ocean of mystery paddling a leaky raft. Our soul swims lazily alongside, beckoning, "Come on in. The water's fine." And we just paddle harder.

Until we don't. Until we are so tired of the suffering we cause ourselves that we are willing to dive into our fear because we are less afraid of the murky depths than of staying where we are.

And guess what. The water is fine. And so are we.

Reason says, the world is limited in six directions
There is no way out
Love says, there is a way
And I have traveled it many times

~Rumi

Chapter 72

When people do not fear authority
Then great empowerment arises
Without restricting people's lives
Without disturbing their homes
Only with true freedom
Are people free from oppression
Thus the sage is self-aware without self-acclaim
Self-loving without self-elevation
Freely moving without attachment

Chapter 72 Reflections

The characters in the first lines of this chapter can be translated so many ways, it's difficult to settle on a meaning, but the focus seems to be a message about different kinds of power: forceful power imposed from without and natural power arising within. When we do not abdicate our spiritual birthright of inherent autonomy in acquiescence to an external force, we allow the limitless energy of the universe to move in us, through us, and from us into the world. This is not the power of individual will, but rather the power of all creation when our separate will is surrendered in alignment with the natural order of existence.

The immense power of this universal energy is blocked when we succumb to fear. Fear cuts us off from the oneness of being by making us believe that we are alone, separate, weak. It can be a bit intimidating to claim our rightful inheritance of universal power. It seems too much for an individual to handle all alone. That's true; it is too much for a single individual. We might feel overwhelmed. What we need to understand, however, is that we are not in charge of this power. We are stewards, conduits of this amazing energy. And there is nothing to fear.

There is nothing to fear because this energy is not harmful. It can't be harmful because it is the power of love. Thus, it frees rather than restricts. It comforts rather than injures. It supports rather than demands. It is not a license to just do as we please; that would be an extension of individual will taken to extremes, without regard to consequences and impact on others. The power of love, in contrast, brings us into alignment with the interconnectedness of all creation. It operates in natural harmony with our lives, our homes, our families, and our communities.

The description of the sage depicts someone who delights in life, walking humbly in service to others, appreciating the miracle of each moment, trusting the basic goodness of the universe. Without fear of authority or desire to impose authority, the sage moves fluidly, unhindered by attachment or aversion. This is true freedom.

> *The ultimate freedom we have as human beings is the power to select what we will allow or require our minds to dwell upon.*
>
> ~Dallas Willard

Chapter 73

Courage to dare leads to death
Courage to not dare leads to life
One benefits, one harms
The ways of heaven cannot be rejected
Even by the sage
Heaven's Dao strives not
Yet victory is assured
Speaks not
Yet responds impeccably
Summons not
Yet always comes
Heaven's net is wide and vast
Infinitely spacious, holding everything

Chapter 73 Reflections

Both daring and not daring are linked to courage in the opening couplet. The distinction is not about having courage, but rather how that courage is directed. In a culture that values bold initiative, this might sound like a play-it-safe admonition. However, the character for daring can also mean to presume, so in this context, the meaning is probably closer to the idea of interfering, or forcing one's will on people or circumstances.

Such daring is always rooted in fear. Because it opposes our true nature, which would always be in alignment with the natural order of the universe, it drains our energy and disconnects us from our innate life force. Courage not to dare or presume, on the other hand, transcends fear and allows the power of creation to course through us and manifest into the world. We are aligned, filled with light, effortlessly experiencing and expressing the life energy that is our true being.

The rest of the chapter reassures us that we need not be concerned. All is well. It cannot be otherwise. When we are aligned with the natural order, we rest in awareness of the perfection of everything. Even if we are not aware, it changes nothing. We are held in heaven's net, connected, secure, loved.

The last two lines remind me of Indra's net, connecting everything in the universe in one vast web, with a jewel at each intersection of the strands, each jewel reflecting the beauty of all other jewels. Like these jewels, we are all connected to all creation, held in infinite embrace, reflecting to all others the divine spark shining within each of us.

You don't know anything
You don't need to know anything
I've got this

~the Universe

Chapter 74

If people have no fear of death
How can death be used to threaten them
When people fear death
They comply with laws strictly enforced
Such enforcement disturbs the natural order
And brings injury to those
Who wield power that is not theirs

Chapter 74 Reflections

What is born in time will end in time. When we can make peace with the inevitable demise of our bodies, we are liberated from fear. The story is told of a monk facing a marauding soldier. The soldier brandished his sword and yelled, "Don't you know I can run you through with this sword without blinking an eye?" When the monk calmly replied, "Don't you know I can be run through with your sword without blinking an eye?" the soldier dropped his sword and fell to his knees, begging to be the monk's disciple. So who had the true power in this story?

In contrast, fear disconnects us from the natural power that courses through us when we are aligned with the flow of energy in the universe. We often seek to escape our fear by attempts to control our circumstances or other people. We can usually justify our efforts by believing that we have no choice, or that our motivation is to help someone or improve the situation. But when we are honest, we admit that we are trying to make ourselves feel better. This is not the way of nature. Furthermore, it is rarely successful, or if it is, the success doesn't last and requires ongoing effort to maintain. This is because we are basing our well-being on things we can't control, and the effort is stressful and exhausting.

There is, however, a better way, suggested by the opening lines of this chapter. Instead of trying to control our external circumstances, we can turn our attention inward. We can recognize and accept the fluid movement of all creation, always changing, always manifesting and returning in cyclic rhythm. We might not be able to face a sword-brandishing marauder without blinking, but perhaps we can give up the exhausting and futile quest to be in charge of everything and everyone, and instead allow this natural energy of creation to move freely in us and through us. Even for a moment. We might find it wondrously magnificent instead of scary and threatening.

A moment of radical acceptance is a moment of genuine freedom.
~Tara Brach

Chapter 75

When rulers tax too much
People starve
When rulers interfere too much
People rebel
When rulers demand too much
People give up
Those who live in harmony with life
Enjoy true wealth

Chapter 75 Reflections

This chapter is about control. Passages in the *Dao De Jing* about governance can apply literally to a government but are perhaps even more helpful in a personal context. After all, we are the rulers of our own lives. The message of this chapter is simple: We create imbalance in our lives through excessive control.

When we look around at our lives and our communities, we see too many layers of regulation – the external control of laws and moral codes, and the internal control of self-improvement and self-judgment. In our constant struggle to do better and be better, we have lost our connection to the natural energy that permeates all of creation, and in doing so, we drain ourselves of our vital life force.

Nature is inherently balanced and self-correcting. When we stand, our bodies are always making microadjustments to keep us vertically aligned. We don't consciously direct our bodies to do this, nor do we calibrate the needed corrections and send instructions to various joints and muscles. Balance is our natural state, and it is naturally maintained. Imagine what would happen if that were not the case.

We take this kind of balance for granted. We trust our bodies to take care of certain functions without our interference. Yet we are hesitant to trust nature in general and our own nature in particular. We have become so distanced from nature's harmony and rhythm that we no longer hear its wisdom and guidance. We no longer sense when we are out of alignment, and if we do become aware, we seek to restore alignment by the very same controlling methods that got us out of alignment in the first place.

We don't need to change who we are; we just need to be who we are. We need to release the fear that we are never quite good enough and trust that who we are is exactly who we need to be. The strain of trying to be something else is wearing us out. Instead, we can explore the fear that blocks our trust. No need to judge the fear or ourselves. We can get to know the fear and the trust. Let them teach us. Let them show us the way home.

You are the universe experiencing itself.
~Alan Watts

Chapter 76

A person at birth is soft and supple
At death is hard and rigid
Sprouting plants are tender and pliant
With age becoming dry and withered
Stiff and unyielding accompany death
Yielding and gentle accompany life
An army that marches only forward is defeated
A tree that does not bend is broken
Those who insist with force are overcome
By those who respond with kindness

Chapter 76 Reflections

The wisdom in this chapter is easy to observe. Babies learning to walk often fall yet are rarely injured. Their bones are flexible. They are unafraid in their efforts so they stay relaxed. Older people can also be unsteady on their feet, but their bones are no longer pliable. They are afraid of injury from a fall so they are more tense, which might contribute to the very injury they are trying to avoid.

We can see this contrast by comparing the characters for supple and rigid. The character for soft, tender, or supple 柔 breaks down into the radical underneath meaning tree 木 and the top part meaning spear. We know that a tree able to bend will survive a storm better than a tree that is stiff. And a spear, even though a strong weapon, has a little give in it to make it more effective.

The character for rigid, brittle, withered 枯 also has the tree radical, this time on the left, while the right part means ancient, suggesting a tree that has lost its flexibility and thus its ability to withstand strong winds.

I witnessed the truth in this chapter, watching an 80-year-old taiji master, small in stature, easily deflect attacks from younger, stronger kung fu teachers. His power came from being relaxed and centered, yielding and fluid. He was unafraid, fully present, responsive rather than reactive. He didn't meet force with force but allowed force to pass by him or through him as he remained unaffected. What I noticed most was that he was having a great time.

Not all of us are taiji masters, but all of us can be life masters. When we encounter the inevitable challenges of life, how do we respond? We can feed the energy of division and hostility with fear, expressing rigid opinions, insisting on being right, or demanding that others conform to our expectations. Or we can feed the energy of mastery. We can pause and breathe, letting the fear move through us or past us, remaining open and receptive, curious, adaptable, responsive to the moment.

When I was young, I memorized this litany against fear. I still find it helpful:

I must not fear. Fear is the mind-killer. Fear is the little-death that brings total obliteration. I will face my fear. I will permit it to pass over me and through me. And when it has gone past I will turn the inner eye to see its path. Where the fear has gone there will be nothing. Only I will remain.

~Frank Herbert, *Dune*

Chapter 77

Heaven's Dao is like stretching a bow
The top is pulled down
The bottom is raised
Heaven's Dao reduces excess
And supplements deficiency
The way of people is not always so
They take from those who have too little
And give to those who have too much
But those who follow Dao
Offer what they have to all under heaven
Thus the sage acts without demand
And succeeds without pride
Having no desire
The sage sees what is truly valuable

Chapter 77 Reflections

This chapter describes two cultural approaches to wealth. In a broader sense, it speaks to nature's self-regulating maintenance of balance and harmony. In a personal context, it speaks to our own internal alignment and equanimity.

The first approach is compared to stringing a bow. The top and bottom are pulled toward each other to allow the string to be looped over the ends, thus creating balance and distributing energy evenly. Some Native American tribes practice a ritual redistribution of wealth. On certain occasions, those who have more generously give to those who have less. Harmonious balance is valued and maintained in the social structure. This mirrors nature's self-correction of imbalance within ecosystems to restore equilibrium. It reminds me of the meditation instruction: "not too tight, not too loose."

A different approach is followed in cultures that allow and even encourage individuals, whether human or corporate, to accumulate unlimited wealth while others live in poverty. Imbalance inevitably results, necessitating legal support to enforce and maintain an artificial and unequal structure, leading to social unrest and discord.

We can see these two approaches reflected in our own lives, not only with respect to wealth, but more generally in how we recalibrate excess and deficiency to establish and maintain inner balance and harmony. Our own internal nature, like nature in the broader sense, seeks equilibrium. Always wanting more – whether that is wealth, love, security, or anything else – or fearing that we have less, leads to chronic discontent and anxiety about acquiring more and defending what we have. When we are out of alignment with our soul values, we suffer internal conflict and stress.

We restore our inner balance and live in harmony by cultivating honest self-awareness without judgment and with compassion. This allows our inner alignment to self-correct just like nature does. So relax, take a breath, and rest in excellence.

Happiness is not a matter of intensity but of balance and order and rhythm and harmony.

~Thomas Merton

Chapter 78

Nothing is more soft and yielding than water
Yet for overcoming what is hard and stiff
Nothing can compare
It is without equal
Supple overcomes stiff
Tender overcomes hard
All under heaven know this
But few can live it
Thus the sage says
Embrace humility to attain mastery
Accept what is to be at peace
Truth appears as paradox

Chapter 78 Reflections

As we approach the end of the *Dao De Jing's* 81 chapters, the text returns to the theme of water. Water is the most common metaphor for the nature of Dao. It flows effortlessly, humbly seeking the lowest level of the vast sea of unity. It yields to force, yet its power cannot be denied. It moves according to its nature through cycles of manifesting and returning, unconcerned with obstacles, sustaining and nurturing all life.

If we all know this, as the chapter says, why is it so hard to apply this wisdom in our lives? What is it that drives our urge to use force, even when we know that it is not advantageous? Fear. Fear is what takes hold of us and leads us to abandon our greatest strength. Fear might be disguised as anger, righteous indignation, anxiety, duty, allegiance to a cause. Whatever its appearance, fear often tells us to fix something outside ourselves to feel better inside ourselves.

Think of all the times during the day when we experience the urge to control, to manipulate, to react, to coerce. As I write this, I don't have to look very far to remember a moment of judgment, irritation, disappointment, worry. And within all these moments is the desire for things to be different, the desire to make them different. Sometimes what I want to change most is myself, to get relief from the self-criticism that can so easily creep into my thoughts.

It might seem counterintuitive to become softer and more yielding to overcome what we perceive as problems, injustices, or things we want to change. Yet water undeniably demonstrates the power of this truth. I've learned through years of martial arts practice that there is always someone stronger, more skilled in using force than I am. In fact, at my age, that would be most everyone. My strength does not lie in my muscles. It lies in my ability to stay fluid, yielding, responsive. Like water.

Practicing the wisdom of this chapter asks us to breathe into discomfort, to tolerate distress, to be still when fear is urging us to react, to soften our hearts and wait patiently until our way is made clear, to respond with integrity and compassion. To ask ourselves, "What would water do?"

Be like water making its way through cracks. Do not be assertive, but adjust to the object, and you will find a way around or through it. If nothing within you stays rigid, outward things will disclose themselves.

~Bruce Lee

Chapter 79

The resolution of a great conflict
Often leaves lingering resentment
How then is true peace achieved
Sages uphold an agreement
Yet claim no debt from others
Manifesting De they honor their word
Without De people demand that others follow through
Heaven's Dao is without bias
Always joined with those whose hearts are open

Chapter 79 Reflections

This thought-provoking chapter seems to offer a turn-the-other-cheek message. It begins by observing that even after a conflict is settled, some bad feelings can remain. There may be outward peace, but inner peace might still be missing.

When I taught contract law, my students were keen to learn how to draft a contract that would "hold up in court." Not a bad objective, but I encouraged them to aim higher, because if their contract was in litigation, they had already lost even if they won in court. The initiation of an adversarial process would arise only after both parties had lost the benefit of their contractual relationship. I told my students that their highest aspiration should be to negotiate and draft an agreement that both parties would honor and that provided a process for good faith resolution of any issues that might arise.

In contracts and in life, the best way to establish and maintain true peace is to prevent conflict from taking hold in the first place. Of course, we can't control other people's behavior, but we can focus on our own behavior, words, and thoughts. We can maintain our own integrity without regard to a quid pro quo. If taken literally, this sounds like a recipe for being taken advantage of, but I think of it more as an inner orientation. No matter what someone else is up to, I need not allow that to disturb my alignment.

This is demonstrated so beautifully in the line "Heaven's Dao is without bias." Like the sun that graces all with its light and warmth, like the rain that nourishes all without discrimination, Dao has no favorites based on worthiness, and punishes no one. And just as nature's power is never diminished by its universal generosity, we can offer our compassion to all who cross our paths. With open hearts we can experience the blessings of Heaven's Dao.

Having no bias or preference is a great description of *wu wei*, a thematic principle in the *Dao De Jing*. Sometimes mistakenly interpreted as passive nonaction, it is better understood as a ready responsiveness to whatever life brings us. If we have a preference, we might try to force things or people to bend to our will. However, if we greet whatever arises without judgment or reactivity, we are free and able to respond appropriately and in harmony, rather than in conflict and struggle. In this way, we maintain our own inner peace and shine that peace upon the world around us.

*People with good intentions make promises,
but people with good character keep them.*

~unknown

Chapter 80

In a small country with few people
There are countless tools available
Yet they are rarely used
The people respect the cycle of life and death
And do not seek to escape it
Though there are boats and carriages
There is nowhere to go
Though there are weapons and armor
There is no one to fight
People return to simple ways
Enjoying tasty food
Appreciating beautiful clothes
Content in their peaceful homes
Happy in their everyday lives
Neighboring communities are close enough to see
Close enough to hear the dogs and roosters
Yet people get old and die
Without going back and forth

Chapter 80 Reflections

This chapter could have been the theme song of the back to the land movement of my youth. There was a yearning at that time to live a simple life, not just a simple life, but a connected life, connected to the earth and all of nature. Now we are technologically connected through devices, social media, and medical advances. Yet at the same time we see nations and groups of people pulling back to be more isolationist and exclusive, perhaps because the connectedness of the digital age does not meet the soul's need for genuine connection. We are creating a virtual reality, literally and figuratively, that leaves us feeling more disconnected from our bodies, from each other, from the earth, from the sacred.

We have labor saving technology of all sorts, yet we are busier than ever. Our economy is driven by consumerism, based on the message of never having enough. We are obsessed with lack and always wanting more. Not only do we never have enough, but we ourselves are never enough – never smart enough, never beautiful enough, never happy enough, never good enough. Just never enough. And so we do more, buy more, try more, and ultimately fail more to be satisfied. A vicious cycle.

The people in this chapter enjoy their tasty food, appreciate their beautiful clothes, live contentedly in their peaceful homes, and are happy in their everyday lives. The configuration of Chinese characters in these lines raises the question of what comes first. For example, are they content because their homes are peaceful, or are their homes peaceful because they are content?

In other words, are these qualities inherent in the objects, or are the qualities a result of the attitude people have toward these objects? Studies have shown that only 10% of our happiness is related to our external circumstances. The true basis for our happiness is our attitudes and our habitual thinking patterns. If we have an attitude of gratitude and contentment, we are more likely to enjoy our life and the things in it.

This chapter invites us to look at our lives with fresh eyes, without judgment, with curiosity about how contentment and discontent play out in how we experience our world. We can explore the influence of the external values adopted by our families and the larger society. We can choose for ourselves the internal values and attitudes that serve the highest good for ourselves and all the earth.

He who is not content with what he has, would not be content with what he would like to have.

~Socrates

Chapter 81

True words are not always beautiful
Beautiful words are not always true
Kind people do not need to be right
The righteous are not always kind
The wise are unconcerned with winning
Those who seek to win lack wisdom
The sage hoards nothing
But shares with all
And thereby has abundance
Heaven's Dao benefits all without interfering
The sage's Dao does what is needed without striving

Chapter 81 Reflections

This last chapter is an end that does not feel like an end, but rather a return to the beginning. The motion of Dao is cyclical rather than linear. It ends where it begins. This is the way.

The *Dao De Jing* begins with the mystery and paradox of eternal Dao, the gate to enlightenment. And here it ends with a model of living an awakened life, benefiting all without interfering, doing what is needed without striving. The energy of the universe shines like the sun, providing light and warmth to all without judgment, without interfering. The ten thousand things of creation manifest and unfold according to their nature and then return to their source in oneness. All is accomplished without interference or manipulation. It's no accident, I think, that *Star Trek*'s "prime directive" prohibits interference with the natural evolution and development of alien cultures. We know in our own lives that interference, no matter how well-intentioned, often leads to unexpected and undesired results.

Yet noninterference does not mean nonengagement. The sage does what is needed. The key is the absence of striving or contending. Appropriate actions arise naturally and effortlessly when they are in harmony with the movement of Dao's intrinsic energy. Ordinary people sometimes act in extraordinary ways. When asked about their actions, they often say that they didn't think. They just instinctively responded to a perceived need. That is Dao in action. While not always so dramatic, Dao works in our lives the same way when we listen to its quiet voice and allow ourselves to be guided by its powerful current.

When we self-reflect, we can see that most of our effort and striving happens in our thinking minds, when we are struggling with what is, wanting something to be different, wanting someone to be different, wanting ourselves to be different. When we contend with reality, we will always lose. But when we loosen our grip and release our insistence, when we trust that we will not be led astray but will be guided truly and unerringly on the path with heart, our way becomes clear in its own time, and we follow its path or rather are carried along its path with effortless energy.

Thus we come full circle in this ancient wisdom teaching. The first chapter of the *Dao De Jing* ends with the character for doorway or gate 门, inviting us to enter the experience of an awakened life, lived fully and in harmony with the natural expression of creation. This last chapter reveals how life unfolds beautifully and perfectly when we step through the door.

The end of all our exploring will be to arrive where we started and know the place for the first time.

~T. S. Eliot

About the Author and Artists

Galen Pearl is a spiritual guide, teacher, student, martial artist, writer, retired law professor, explorer of the *Dao De Jing* and other wisdom teachings, and embracer of life's mystery. For more information about her books and access to her blog, please visit galenpearl.com.

Lydia Pallas Loren is a mother, grandmother, law professor, and amateur naturalist. She likes to wander in nature, marveling at the many manifestations of the energy of the universe, and welcomes opportunities to share images of the beautiful things she witnesses.

Martha Spence is a retired waitress, file clerk, and law school administrator. She is especially attracted to what images can offer as a way into the teachings of the Dao.

www.ingramcontent.com/pod-product-compliance
Lightning Source LLC
Chambersburg PA
CBHW062056290426
44110CB00022B/2616